JESUS IS GOD

CLEAR ANSWERS FROM THE BIBLE CONCERNING:

Does the Bible teach the Deity of Jesus? What is the meaning of Jesus' name? Why was Jesus called Emmanuel? The Impeccability of Christ! Could Jesus sin? And much more......

BY

Dennis D. Helton

Library of Congress Control Number: 2009922534
REL006000: Religion: Biblical Studies - General

ISBN 978-0-9820608-8-9

All Scripture quotes are from the King James Bible

Address All Inquiries To:
THE OLD PATHS PUBLICATIONS, Inc.
142 Gold Flume Way
Cleveland, Georgia, U.S.A.

Web: www.theoldpathspublications.com
E-mail: TOP@theoldpathspublications.com

1.0

DEDICATION

This work is dedicated to my six daughters Debbie, Donna, Dale, Denise, Deree, and Dena whom I love very much.

"For by grace are ye saved through faith; and that not of yourselves: *it is* the gift of God: Not of works, lest any man should boast."

Ephesians 2:8-9

JESUS IS GOD

Clear Answers From The Bible To The Following Questions (And Many More):

- Does the Bible teach the Deity of **Jesus**?

- What is the meaning of **Jesus' name**?

- Why was **Jesus** called **Emmanuel**?

- The **Impeccability of Christ**! Could Jesus sin?

- Is **Jesus The Only Way** to Heaven?

- Did **God c**all **Jesus, "God**?"

- Is **Jesus** equal to **God t**he Father?

- Did **Jesus** prove that He is **Messiah**?

- Is **Jesus a** created being as Arianism claims?

- Who are they that deny **The Son**?

- Is God "**The Word,**" in John 1:1?

- Is the **I AM** of the OT the **I AM** of the NT?

"For God so loved the world, that he gave his only begotten Son, that whosoever believeth in him should not perish, but have everlasting life."

John 3:16

PREFACE

Why the Use of "IS" in the Book Title:

The observant reader will notice the use of the present-tense verb "Is" in the title of this writing. Of course, the writer uses the present-tense verb *is* arbitrarily because it best expresses continuance; Jesus is God, Jesus has always been God, and Jesus will always be God.

The inactive verb "was" might suggest non-continuance to the unlearned and Jesus will never cease to be God.

The inactive verbs "will be" are inaccurate because their usage would deny the eternal beginning of Christ.

"Jesus Is God" best expresses Jesus' eternal past Deity with God the Father, His present Deity with His Father, and His everlasting Deity with God the Father that They may be all in one (1 John 5:7). To the unsuspecting and naïve, the verb tenses "was," and "will be" might erroneously suggest that Jesus is not God. Actually, all three verb tenses may accurately express the Deity of Jesus in the proper context: Jesus *was* God; Jesus *is* God; Jesus always *will be* God. The writer will try to extol the glory of God and the Deity of His Son in this writing.

Why This Writing?

There are many religious professors, religious sects, cultists, phony ministers, and even Jews of Jesus' own people that deny the Deity of Christ (the Jews are still anticipating the First Coming of Messiah). Many ignoramus religious unbelievers also boldly make the false claim that the Bible nowhere substantiates the Deity of Christ. Even some students of the Bible state that Jesus nowhere claimed Deity. What have they been reading, "funny" books? The writer is ashamed to admit that he has only read the Bible through about twenty times (not counting untold hours of studying), but he had no trouble at all finding absolutely overwhelming evidence from Scriptures of Christ's Deity in his first reading. Not only does the Bible teach the Deity of Christ but Jesus Himself claimed to be the Son of God. The deniers of Christ's Deity loudly advertise their gross ignorance of the Scriptures. The Bible (KJV) readily exposes the false claims of the unbelievers.

> **John 8:24:** *"I said therefore unto you, that ye shall die in your sins: for if ye believe not that I am he, ye shall die in your sins." (Cf. with I John 2:1-2, 22-23; 3:16; 4:1-3, 14-15; 5:1, 5, 10-11, 20."*

Christianity is Valid Only if Jesus is God Manifest in the Flesh

To the **true** Christian, there is no doubt that Jesus is God who came from Heaven to earth to take upon Himself the form of a man. God was manifest in the flesh that He may die as a sacrifice for the sin of the whole world.

> **John 3:16:** *"For God so loved the world, that he gave his only begotten Son, that whosoever believeth in him should not perish, but have everlasting life."*

Amazingly, there are many who claim to be of God and yet reject the Deity of Jesus Christ. The very basis of Christianity rests solely upon whether or not Jesus is God come in human form, incarnate in a body of flesh. If Jesus is anything less than Deity (God) in flesh, the claims of Christianity have no basis.

(<u>True</u> – It is necessary to say "true" Christian because there are multitudes falsely claiming to be Christians who are not genuine. They are Christian in name only.)

"Verily, verily, I say unto you, He that heareth my word, and believeth on him that sent me, hath everlasting life, and shall not come into condemnation; but is passed from death unto life."

John 5:24

TABLE OF CONTENTS

"My sheep hear my voice, and I know them, and they follow me: And I give unto them eternal life; and they shall never perish, neither shall any man pluck them out of my hand. My Father, which gave them me, is greater than all; and no man is able to pluck them out of my Father's hand."

John 10:27-29

CHAPTER 1

GOD BECAME MAN

What do the Scriptures Say About God Condescending to the Form of a Man?

*I Timothy 3:16: And without controversy great is the mystery of godliness: **God was manifest in the flesh**, justified in the Spirit, seen of angels, preached unto the Gentiles, believed on in the world, received up into glory.*

Jesus is "God manifest in the flesh" and the only person who ever lived, or ever will live, that fulfills I Timothy 3:16. If Jesus is not God, then no one is saved, all Christians are under strong delusion, and we just die as dogs and cats. However, the Scriptures dogmatically teach that Jesus is God and genuine Christians know "**...in whom they have believed...**" – (**2 Timothy** 1:12; **Romans** 4:21).

Mary's Virgin Born Son is Declared to be God with us

*Matthew 1:23: "Behold, a virgin shall be with child, and shall bring forth a **Son (Jesus),** and they shall call his name **Emmanuel**, which being interpreted is, **God with us.**"*

This verse may be too hard to grasp for false religionists and some "so-called" deep theologians, but a child can easily understand the meaning (without understanding the "how"). Matthew 1:23 interprets itself.

There are many that say that Jesus was fully man, but not divine. Some say He was fully God but not man. The **Gnostics** wanted to make Him into a divine spirit who was not really connected to the physical world.

Gnosticism

Gnosticism is a system of mystical religious and philosophical doctrines, stressing gnosis (knowledge of spiritual things, especially a secret and superior knowledge limited to an elite few, such as the Gnostics claimed to have) as essential to salvation, viewing matter as evil, and variously combining ideas derived from mythology, ancient Greek philosophy, ancient religions, and eventually Christianity. (*Webster's New World College Dictionary*, Fourth Edition, © 2004 by Wiley Publishing, Inc., Cleveland, Ohio.)

Jesus was fully man and fully God at the same time. The act of God of taking upon Himself a body of flesh and blood is referred to by theologians as "hypostasis" (pronounced, "hī´ pas´tă sǐs"). The hypostatic union of Deity and humanity is also called "incarnation" meaning "enfleshment," the act of assuming bodily form.

What Does "Jesus" and "Christ" Mean?

Jesus is the Greek equivalent of the Hebrew word **Joshua** (Yeshua) meaning **Savior** - (**Matthew** 1:21). Jesus refers particularly to the Lord's humanity and incarnation by which He became a man in order to die for every man's sins.

Christ is the Greek equivalent of the Hebrew word **Messiah**, meaning **anointed**, and refers to Jesus as the Messiah who was promised in OT Scripture - (**Daniel** 9:25-26; **John** 1:14; 4:25; **Acts**

2:36). Christ refers particularly to the Lord's **eternal** deity as the **Son of God.**

JESUS IS GOD Manifest in the Flesh

Again, there is no other person who ever lived in this world that could satisfy the following Scripture than the Lord Jesus Christ Himself:

> *I Timothy 3:16:* "And without controversy great is the mystery of godliness: **God was manifest in the flesh,** justified in the Spirit, seen of angels, preached unto the Gentiles, believed on in the world, received up into glory."

It could not be any clearer than this, "**God** was manifest in the **flesh** (bodily)!" God entered the kingdom of man so that man might enter the kingdom of God. Others express God's grace in another beautiful way, "The Son of God became the Son of man so that the sons of men might become the Sons of God."

Actually, further exposition is not necessary. Enough Scriptures has already been shown to convince any reasonable person that the Bible teaches the Deity of Christ. However, in hope of convincing the slow-witted and the unbelieving proud intellectual, the writer will continue this brief exposition.

In Heaven, Jesus could not die. **The Son of God**, who could not die without an earthly body, became **The Son of Man** on earth so that He could die for sinners.

> *Hebrews 2:9:* "But we see Jesus who was made a little lower than the angels for the suffering of death, crowned with glory and honour; that he by the grace of God should taste death for every man."

Here, as in John 3:16, we have the promise of God, a provision of salvation for "every man." As the Son of God in Heaven, Jesus could not die. Jesus had to become the Son of man in order to die. He had to take upon Himself a body of flesh and become a man. Jesus came to earth to die a perfect sacrifice for whosoever would believe on Him.

Jesus did not begin to exist when He was born of Mary but shared glory with His Father before the world was created.

> **John 17:5:** *"And now, O Father, glorify thou me with thine own glory which I had with thee **before the world was**."*

Jesus came forth from the Father (**John** 16:3, 7, 27-28, 30; 17:1, 3, 5, 8, 22, 24). He returned to His Father after purging our sins.

> **Hebrews 1:3:** *"Who being the brightness of his glory, and the express image of his person and upholding all things by the word of his power, when he had by himself purged our sins, **sat down on the right hand of the Majesty on high**."*

No one could qualify to sit down at God's throne except he be Deity Himself. Moses could not; neither Elijah, Isaiah, Jeremiah, Daniel, Joseph, Peter, Paul, John, nor Mary. Neither could Angels ascend to such a glorious position even though Lucifer, through his **pride** desired worship as God.

> **Isaiah 14:13-15:** *"For thou (King of Babylon; **Lucifer**; son of the morning; the Assyrian) has said in thine heart, **I will** ascend into heaven, **I will** exalt my throne above the stars of God; **I will** sit also upon the mount of the congregation, in the sides of the north: **I will** ascend above the heights of the clouds; **I will** be like the most High. Yet thou shalt be brought down to hell, to the sides of the pit."*

Observe the prideful *"I will's."* God does not share his throne with any of his creatures.

Actually, there are 21 references in Scriptures to Christ being at the right hand of the Father. The first is in Psalms 16:8. There are five in Hebrews (1:3; 8:1; 10:12; 12:2). Jesus is our *"...great high priest, that is passed into the heavens, Jesus the Son of God..."* –**Hebrews** 4:14.

What is the Meaning of *"this day have I begotten thee"* in Hebrews 1:5?

Hebrews 1:5: *"For unto which of the angels said he at any time, Thou art my Son, **this day have I begotten thee?** And again, I will be to him a Father, and he shall be to me a Son."*

Some Bible students and theologians alike believe this to be in reference to Christ's birth; however, Jesus has always existed with the Father and was not begotten or begun to exist at His birth. The writer believes that *"this day have I begotten thee"* is reference to Christ's resurrection from the dead.

Actually, the great means by which Christ is declared to be the Son of God is by His resurrection from the dead. The resurrection of Jesus (not His birth) is also referred to in Psalms, Acts, and Colossians.

Romans 1:4: *"And declared to be the Son of God with power, according to the spirit of holiness, **by the resurrection** form the dead."*
Acts 13:33: *"God hath fulfilled the same unto us their children, in that he hath **raised up Jesus** again; as it is also written in the second psalm, Thou art my Son, **this day have I begotten thee."***
Psalms 2:7: *"I will declare the decree: the LORD hath said unto me, Thou art my Son; **this day have I Begotten thee**."*

> **Colossians 1:18:** *"And he is the head of the body, the church: who is the beginning, **the firstborn from the dead**; that in all things he might have the preeminence."*

NOTE: The writer is not trying to split theological hairs [as the old proverbial argument of how many angels could stand upon the point of a needle]. The writer is simply stating his understanding of the of the meaning of Hebrews 1:5 as to be in reference to the resurrection of Jesus rather than that of His birth.

God sent Gabriel to Explain to Mary That Her Son Would Be His Son

> **Luke 1:31-35:** *"And, behold, thou shalt conceive in thy womb, and bring forth a son, and shalt call his name **JESUS**. He shall be great, and shall be called **the Son of the Highest**: and the Lord God shall give unto him the throne of his father David: And he shall reign over the house of Jacob for ever; and of his kingdom there shall be no end. Then said Mary unto the angel, How shall this be, seeing I know not a man? And the angel answered and said unto her, **The Holy Ghost** shall come upon thee, and the power of the Highest shall overshadow thee: therefore also that holy thing which shall be born of thee shall be called **the Son of God**."*

This is plain language and must be received by faith in God's promise of sending forth His Son, the promised Messiah.

Some Claim that Numbers 23:19 Disprove the Deity of Christ:

> **Numbers 23:19:** *"God is not a man, that he should lie; neither the son of man that he should repent: hath he said, and shall he not do it? Or hath he spoken, and shall he not make it good?"*

Numbers 23:19 does not disprove "The Incarnation" but it does show the necessity of the incarnation. Jesus was not just a man and nothing more. Though Jesus was a man, He never ceased to be God. It was absolutely necessary for God to come to earth as a man and shed His blood for the remission of our sins. That is why He became a man. There is no other person or entity (man; angel; phony god; idol; demon) in the entire universe worthy to pay a ransom for our sin.

Although Jesus set aside His glory and limited Himself upon His First Coming on earth, He never ceased to be God incarnate in flesh and retained the power to do miracles. Neither did He make His path easy by using His creation power. When Jesus had **hungered** after fasting forty days and forty nights, the devil tempted Him to turn stones into **bread**. Jesus refused and told the tempter that *"man shall not live by bread alone but by every Word that proceedeth out of the mouth of God"* (**Matthew** 4:1-4).

Jesus could have anesthetized Himself to avoid the horrible pain and sufferings but He chose to suffer the **full** brunt of sin that man deserved (God's holiness and righteous judgment demanded **full** payment for sin). Again, Jesus retained His Divine power while in the flesh and was not limited to 'just a great man' and nothing more.

A clever person can twist and put a spin upon Scriptures to prove almost anything they want.

During trial, the high priest asked Jesus if He was the Christ:

> **Mark 14:61-b, 62:** *"...Again the high priest asked him, and said unto him,* **Art thou the Christ, the Son of the Blessed?** *And* **Jesus said, I am:** *and ye shall see the Son of man sitting on the right hand of power, and coming in the clouds of heaven."*

Again, in order for lost men to be *reconciled* (bring into harmony) to God, Jesus, being God, had to take upon Himself **a body of flesh** in order to taste death for every man:

Colossians 1:22: "*In the body of his flesh through death*, to present you holy and unblameable and unreproveable in his sight:"

Hebrews 10:19-20: "Having therefore, brethren, boldness to enter into the holiest *by the blood of Jesus*. By a new and living way, which he hath consecrated for us, through the veil, that is to say, *his flesh.*"

Since sin entered the world by man, it must be by man that he is to be redeemed:

Romans 5:12: "Wherefore, as by one man sin entered into the world, and death by sin; and so death passed upon all men, for that all have sinned."

Romans 5:18-19: "Therefore as by the offence of one judgment came upon all men to condemnation; even so by the righteousness of one the free gift came upon all men unto justification of life. For as by one man's disobedience many were made sinners, so by the obedience of one shall man be made righteous."

Since angels do not die, Jesus took upon Himself a body of flesh and became a man:

Hebrews 2:14, 16-17: "Forasmuch then as the children are partakers of flesh and blood, *he also himself likewise took part of the same*; that through death he might destroy him that had the power of death, that is, the devil; For verily *he took not on him the nature of angels*; but he took on him the seed of Abraham. Wherefore in all things it *behoved him to be made like unto his brethren*, that he might be a merciful and faithful high priest in things pertaining to God, to make reconciliation for the sins of the people."

God's Love for Fallen Sinful Man is Wonderfully Expressed in John's Gospel:

John 3:16: *"For* **G***od so loved the world, that he gave his* **O***nly begotten* **S***on, that whosoever believeth in him should not* **P***erish, but have* **E***verlasting* **L***ife."*

In John 3:16, it is interesting to note the acrostic, "G-O-S-P-E-L." Some refer to John 3:16 as "The Gospel in a Nutshell."

Someone has explained the message of John 3:16 in terms of "The Greatest:"

◆   *For God* - "The Greatest lover"

◆   *So loved* - "The Greatest degree of love"

◆   *The World* - "The Greatest company"

◆   *That He gave* - "The Greatest act"

◆   *His Only Begotten Son* - "The Greatest gift"

◆   *That whosoever* - "The Greatest invitation"

◆   *Believeth* - "The Greatest simplicity"

◆   *In Him* - "The Greatest attraction"

◆   *Should not perish* - "The Greatest promise"

◆   *But* - "The Greatest difference"

◆   *Have* - "The Greatest assurance"

◆   *Everlasting Life* - "The Greatest possession"

*"All things are of God, who hath reconciled us to Himself by Jesus Christ "- (**II Corinthians** 5:14-21.* *See also **Mark** 10:45; **Romans** 5:8-9, 18-21; **I Timothy** 2:5-6; **Hebrews** 2:17; 10:4-12; **I John** 3:5.)*

What do People of Phony Religions Falsely Claim Against Jesus Christ?

➢   The people of the **Jesus Only** sect say that Jesus only is God. This is a denial of the Tri-Unity of God...**God the Father,**

God the Son, and God the Holy Spirit. Virtually every cult is Unitarian in theology.

➢ Some **Seventh-Day Adventist** preachers have been guilty of declaring publicly that before His birth, Jesus Christ was Michael the Archangel, thus making Him less than God, a creature of God.

➢ The **Jehovah Witness's** (*Paradise Lost and Paradise Regained*) have a similar view of Jesus as the Seventh-Day Adventists. They claim that Jesus is the brother of Michael the Archangel.

➢ **Islam** teaches that Jesus was only a good prophet, but not the Son of God. Their Koran says that Allah had no son. Of course, their Allah is the ancient moon-god of Persia, not the God of the Bible. Islam teaches that Muhammad is the final great prophet.

➢ **Mormons** teach that Jesus was a good prophet but believe that Joseph Smith to be a later prophet fulfilling what Jesus was "unable to accomplish." They also teach that God was once a man and then became God. They got it backwards, the proverbial "cart before the horse." Man cannot become God. God became man in the person of His Son Jesus Christ and He never ceased to be God.

➢ **Roman Catholicism** accepts the Deity of Jesus but idolize Mary as a "go between, co-redemptress" with Christ and "intercessor" to God. They claim that Mary was born without sin and entered into Heaven without sin, usurping the glory of God's Son, the Lord Jesus Christ. Prayers to the blessed Mary go no higher than the ceiling. Undoubtedly, Mary herself would be greatly shocked at such idolatry.

➢ **Modernism** is a false religion that denies the deity of Christ. Compare Isaiah 44:6 to Revelation 22:13.

The writer makes no apology for pointing out the errors of false religions. It was apostate Jewish religionists that demanded the crucifixion of The Son of God. Even today, many unbelieving Jews have not understood why they have suffered atrocities.

Any person or nation that rejects the claims of Jesus Christ will eventually suffer the judgment of God. False religions owe repentance and apology to Christ and His Word.

Jesus Never Ceased to be God

As a man, Jesus limited himself from his divine rights upon His First Coming upon the earth, but He never ceased to be God.

If Jesus were not all man, He would be only half-man; if Jesus were not all God, He would only be half-God. Jesus was not half-man and half-God. **Jesus was All-Man and All-God at the same time.** The writer does not claim to fully comprehend this miraculous truth. How can a *finite* creature fully understand his *infinite* **Creator**? Jesus was born with the essence of two natures:

1. Humanity (a body – **Hebrews 10:5**; but without sin – **2 Corinthians 5:21**) and

2. Divinity (conceived of the Holy Ghost – **Matthew 1:18, 20**). Jesus is the God-man. It is said only of Jesus, *"conceived of the Holy Ghost."*

It was not so much Jesus' virgin **birth** that was miraculous (and it was), but His conception. Jesus was born of a natural birth (but His birth **was** miraculous in the sense that He had no natural father) and with the human body by his mother Mary (He thirsted, hungered, and felt pain). Jesus' **conception** by the Holy Spirit was miraculous and He also possessed the Divine nature of His Father. Jesus was both 100 % man and 100 % God at the same time.

Unless Jesus was perfect man (God-man), He could not die for our sins. Unless Jesus was God, He could not defeat death and Hell and could not save us.

The Kinsman-Redeemer

The redemption of man by God is beautifully illustrated by the earthly Kinsman-Redeemer of Old Testament teaching.

In order for the Israelite to be redeemed out of servitude and be set free, there were three necessary qualifications for the one who would redeem him:

1. The redeemer had to be a near kinsman - (Our Saviour became perfect man).
2. The redeemer had to be able to redeem – (Jesus owns all power and wealth).
3. The redeemer had to be willing to redeem – (Jesus proved that on the Cross)

There was a day in history when God left His glorious throne in Heaven and descended to earth to become a man (God-man; our Kinsman-Redeemer), but there was never a time in history when God began to be God:

> *Job 38:4:* "Where wast thou when I laid the foundations of the earth? declare, if thou hast understanding."
> *I Timothy 3:16:* "...great is the mystery of godliness: God was manifest in the flesh."

In the Gospel of John , the Word is "God," Not "a God."

The **Word** (**Jesus**) was always God and will always be God.

One false religion (Jehovah Witnesses) claims that John 1:1 says, "The Word was **a** God" instead of, *"The Word was God."*

John 1:1: *In the beginning was the Word and the Word was with God, and the Word was God.*

The Greek Text Reads Like This (Berry's Greek Testament):

John 1:1: *"In [the] beginning was the Word, and the Word was with God, and God was the Word."*

In John 1:1:

-subject = the Word

-verb = was

-predicate nominative = God

Greek scholars say that it is not necessary to translate Greek nouns that have **no** definite article (definite article "the" = Greek "ho") with an indefinite article (a) as in **"...and the Word was God."** There is no indefinite article (a) in the Greek of **"...and the Word was"** of **John 1:1**.

A "predicative nominative" of a sentence is identical to the "noun subject."

Not only is Jesus called **The Word of God** in John 1:1 but John 1:14 says. "...The Word was made flesh (His incarnation into the human race – **Hebrews 2:14-17**), and dwelt among us..." Jesus' name is called **The Word of God** in Revelation 19:13. Of course, Jesus is the KING OF KINGS AND LORD OF LORDS - (**Revelation 19:16**).

John 1:2: *"The same was in the beginning with God."*
Berry's Greek New Testament reads like this:

John 1:2: "He was in [the] beginning with God.

The Word of God (Jesus) was God, yet also *"with God"* (in a triune sense.). God is both personal and plural (Elohim = Strong's Hebrew #430, espec. plural). The Word of God is used 1,200 times in the Old Testament. In this verse, the definite article "the" was supplied by the translators. So it is *"in beginning"* (en arche) or before the creation of the universe, so that the meaning of John's *"beginning"* even precedes the *"beginning"* of Genesis without an initial beginning into eternity past, before even time was created (John 17:24), *"before the foundation of the world."* John 1:3 says *"all things were made by Him."*

False religionists deny that Jesus is truly God come in the flesh and relegate Him to the level of a mere prophet. They do not understand that any sacrifice offered by a mere prophet or a great man is completely out of the realm of *expiating* (atoning; make amends; pay the penalty; make satisfaction) man's sin and *reconciling* (settle a quarrel; make friendly again; bring into harmony) his sinfulness to God.

The Old Testament sacrifices did not take away sin (**Hebrews 10:4**) but only *atoned* (covered; bring into agreement) man's sin until the perfect sacrifice of Jesus Christ on the cross could pay the final and **full** price that God demanded for payment of sin. The perfect sacrifice of Jesus removed our transgressions from us as far as the east is from the west, never to be remembered against us any more (Psalms 103:12). The shed blood of Jesus Christ washes away our sin (Revelation 1:5), not just covers it for a time only as did the blood of bulls and goats, which could never take away sin (**Hebrews 9:12-14; 10:1, 4**). If Jesus were to be relegated to only an iota less than God, His sacrifice for sin would avail nothing. All that would be left is man's works to pay for his sins.

A person is not saved if they do not believe that Jesus is God - (John 8:24, 28, 32, 46, 47). However, they may be incurably religious!

If Scriptures named Jesus the "Son of God" only once, that would be sufficient proof of His divinity - (*"The Scripture cannot be broken"* - **John 10:35**). Jesus is explicitly called "The Son of God" about 44 times in the NT. Repetition of God's Word is not necessary to establish truth. Jesus claimed to be "The Son of God" so plainly that even unsaved Jewish religious leaders understood Him. The Jews even sought to kill Him because He made Himself equal with God.

> ***John 5:17-18:*** *"But Jesus answered them, My Father worketh hitherto (until now; before) and I work. Therefore the Jews sought the more to kill him, because he not only had broken the sabbath), but said also **that God was his Father making himself equal with God.**"*

The Jew's accusation of Jesus breaking the Sabbath was according to their rules and traditions. The Son of Man came to set men free from man-made rules.

The Book of John, more times than any other book of the Bible, proclaims the Deity of Christ and His salvation. Actually, this was the reason that the book of John was written:

> ***John 20:31:*** *"But these (signs) are written, that ye might believe that **Jesus is the Christ, The Son of God;** and that believing ye might have life through his name."*

The miracles of Jesus and those performed by His apostles authenticated the Gospel of Christ and set it apart from the heathen and false religions of the world.

John, the writer of the Gospel of John, also wrote that the believer can **know** that he has eternal life and that the unbeliever can also believe on the name of the Son of God.

> *I John 5:13:* "these things have I written unto you that believe on the name of the Son of God; that ye may **know** that ye have eternal life, and that ye may believe on the name of the Son of God."

Salvation is not a "hope so," "maybe so," "think so" condition of the soul. Salvation is an absolute "know so" matter. Why would anyone not desire to be absolutely sure about their eternal destiny.

The writer was curious as to how many *"knows"* were in this chapter that gives complete assurance of the believer's soul. The word *"know"* is found seven times, vv. 1, 13, 15, 18-20. Knowing that doctrine is not based upon numbers, it is a blessing to know that the number seven is the biblical number representative of completion and finality. Eternal life is an unconditional gift that is not based upon any kind of works, sacrifices, or sacraments.

There is nothing more important to a person than to have the full assurance (Hebrews 6:11) and **know** that he is saved:

> *I John 3:14:* "We **know** that we have passed from death unto life because we love the brethren..."
> *I John 3:24:* "...And hereby we **know** that he abideth in us, by the Spirit which he hat given us."
> *I John 3:19:* "And hereby we **know** that we are of the truth, and shall assure our hearts before him."
> *I John 4:13:* "Hereby **know** we that we dwell in him, and he in us, because he hath given us of his Spirit."
> *I John 5:1-2:* "Whosoever believeth that Jesus is the Christ is born of God: and everyone that loveth him that begat loveth him also that is begotten of him. By this we **know** that we love the children of God, when we love God, and keep his commandments."
> *I John 5:13:* "These things have I written unto you that believe on the name of the Son of God; that ye may **know** that ye have eternal life, and that ye may believe on the name of the Son of God."
> *I John 5:19:* "And we **know** that we are of God, and the whole world lieth in wickedness."

I John 5:20: "And we **know** that the Son of God is come, and hath given an understanding, that we may **know** him that is true, and we are in him that is true, even in his Son Jesus Christ. This is the true God, and eternal life."

The New Testament Writers Said That Jesus Christ is God

John 1:1, 14: "In the beginning was the Word, and the Word was with God, and **the Word was God**. And **the Word was made flesh**, and **dwelt among us**, (and we beheld his glory, the glory as of the only begotten of the Father,) full of grace and truth."

God, in the person of His Son Jesus Christ, dwelt among men.

Revelation 19:13: "And he was clothed with a vesture dipped in blood: and his name is called **The Word of God**."

Jesus is also called "The Word of God" in John 1:1, 14.

John 1:14: "And the Word was made flesh, and dwelt among us, (and we beheld his glory, the glory as of the only begotten of the Father), full of grace and truth."

It can be no clearer than this, Jesus Christ, the Word of God, who was the promised Messiah, the Son of God, came and dwelt in a body of flesh among His creation.

Acts 29:28, 31: "Be it known therefore unto you, that the salvation of God is sent unto the Gentiles, and that they will hear it. Preaching the kingdom of God, and teaching those things which concern the Lord Jesus Christ, with all confidence, no man forbidding him."

> *Acts 10:36: "The word which God sent unto the children of Israel, preaching peace by Jesus Christ: (he is Lord of all:)"*
> *Philippians 2:5-6: "Let this mind be in you, which was also in **Christ Jesus**: Who, being in the form of God, thought it not robbery to be **equal with God**: But made himself of no reputation, and took upon him the form of a servant, and **was made in the likeness of men."***

Upon earth, Jesus was both God and man at the same time (He set aside the fullness of His glory).

> *Colossians 1:15: "**Who is the image** of the invisible God, the firstborn of every creature."*

While it could be said that a believer should reflect the **image** of God's holiness, nowhere could it be said of any OT or NT saint that they were the image of the invisible God.

> *Colossians 2:9: "For in him (Jesus) dwelleth all the fullness of the **Godhead** bodily."*

The Godhead consisted of God the Father, God the Son, and God the Holy Spirit.

> *I Timothy 3:16: "And without controversy great is the mystery of godliness: **God was manifest in the flesh**, justified in the Spirit, seen of angels, preached unto the Gentiles, believed on in the world, received up into glory."*

We are repeatedly told over and over again that God was manifest in the flesh. Perhaps some of our proud (but dumb) intellectuals have a need to return to elementary grade school to learn basic word definitions.

> *I Timothy 6:14, 16: "That thou keep this commandment without spot, unrebukeable, until the appearing of our Lord Jesus Christ: Who only hath*

immortality, dwelling in the light which no man can approach unto; whom no man hath seen, nor can see: to whom be honour and power everlasting. Amen."
Hebrews 1:3: *"Who being the brightness of his glory, and **the express image** of his person, and upholding all things by the word of his power, when he had by himself purged our sins, **sat down on the right hand of the Majesty on high**."*

Only God the Son could share the throne of God. Lucifer was exiled from Heaven for his wishful thinking.

Titus 2:13: *"Looking for that blessed hope, and the glorious appearing of the great God and our Saviour Jesus Christ."*

The great God and our Saviour Jesus Christ are one and the same.

I John 3:16: *"Hereby perceive we **the love of God, because he laid down his life for us**: and we ought to lay down our lives for the brethren."*

How could God lay down His life (die) for us? God knew the perfect answer. He had to take upon Himself a body of flesh. The Word (God the Son; Jesus) was made flesh – **John 1:1, 14.**

"Looking for that blessed hope, and the glorious appearing of the great God and our Saviour Jesus Christ;"

Titus 2:13

CHAPTER 2

JESUS CLAIMS TO BE GOD

The High Priests, Elders, and Scribes Understood Jesus' Claim to be the Son of God:

Matthew 26:63-65: *"But Jesus held his peace. And the high priest answered and said unto him, I adjure thee by the living God, that thou **tell us whether thou be the Christ, the Son of God. Jesus saith unto him, Thou has said:** nevertheless I say unto you, Hereafter shall ye see the Son of man sitting on the right hand of power, and coming in the clouds of heaven. Then the high priest rent his clothes, saying, He hath spoken blasphemy; what further need have we of witnesses? Behold, now ye have heard his blasphemy."*

Mark 14:61-62: *"But he held his peace, and answered nothing. Again the high priest asked him, and said unto him, **Art thou the Christ, the Son of the Blessed?** And **Jesus said, I am:** and ye shall see the Son of man sitting on the right hand of power, and coming in the clouds of heaven."*

Again, the high priest understood Jesus' claim to be the Son of God. See also Luke 22:70-71; 23:2; John 19:7.

On Another Occasion, It Was Certain in the Minds of Unsaved Jews That Jesus Claimed to be God:

John 10:33: *"The Jews answered him, saying, For a good work we stone thee not; but for blasphemy; and because that thou, being a man, makest thyself God."*

Nowhere does Jesus ever disclaim His Deity. All of the unbelieving Jews acknowledged Jesus' claim of Deity. That is why they accused Him of blasphemy! If they simply misunderstood Jesus' claim of Deity, then why didn't Jesus correct them? If Jesus had not been God and remained silent concerning the charges of His Deity, He would not have been a good man or great prophet (of which the cults relegate Him).

On Another Occasion, Unsaved Jews Understood That Jesus Claimed Deity

John 5:18: "*Therefore the Jews sought the more to kill him, because he not only had broken the Sabbath, but said also that God was his Father, **making himself equal with God.**"*

Of Course, the Apostle Paul Taught the Divinity of Jesus

*Philippians 2:6-7: **Who, being in the form of God,** thought it not robbery to be **equal with God**: But made himself of no reputation, and took upon him the form of a servant, and **was made in the likeness of men**.*

How is it that a child can understand the Deity of Christ but cultists and many theologians cannot?

I Corinthians 2:14-15 "*The natural man (unregenerate) receiveth not the things of the Spirit of God...*"
*Romans 3:3-4: "For what **if some did not believe**? Shall their unbelief make the faith of God without effect? God forbid: yea, let God be true, but every man a liar; as it is written, That thou mightest be justified in thy sayings, and mightest overcome when thou art judged.*"

John 4:48: "Then said Jesus unto him, Except ye see signs and wonders, ye will not **believe**."

The Demons Recognized
the Deity of Jesus

Matthew 8:29: "And, behold, they (demons; devils) cried out, saying, What have we to do with thee, **Jesus, thou Son of God**? Art thou come hither to torment us before the time?"

The devils themselves acknowledged Christ's Deity calling Him "Thou Son of God." They acknowledged the power of God and were concerned that they may be tormented before the time. Of course, mere man does not have power to torment demons. Neither does any other entity.

Isaiah's Prophecy:

Isaiah 40:3: "The voice of him that crieth in the wilderness, Prepare ye the way of the LORD, make straight in the desert a highway for our God."

This Messianic prophecy calls The Coming One both *"LORD:"* (Jehovah) and *"God"*

(Elohim), the pre-existent one in eternity (John 1:15), the Lord of life and God of creation. It can easily be seen that Jesus is the fulfillment of this prophecy in the NT – (**John 1:23**).

- ✓ -Andrew knew him (John 1:4)
- ✓ -Philip knew him (John 1:45)
- ✓ -Nathanael knew him (John 1:49)
- ✓ -Thomas knew him (John 20:28)

Jesus Instructed a Man
Who Had Great Possessions:

A wealthy man asked of Jesus, *"Good Master, what good things shall I do, that I may have eternal life?"* – (**Matthew 19:16**). In order to bring the man to a point of decision in acknowledging His Deity as the Son of God, Jesus tells him that if He Himself is just another Jewish rabbi or prophet, then He is not good because only God is truly good. Either Jesus was God and He was good, or He was not God and He was not good. Jesus must be believed on as the Son of God who came forth from His Father. There is no middle ground; neither is there such thing as a true Christian who doesn't believe in the Deity of Christ.

> *I John 5:5:* Who is he that overcometh the world, but he that believeth that *Jesus is the Son of God*?

Dr. Gary Hedrick (President of *CJF Ministries*) says:

> "But let us not come with any patronizing nonsense about his being a great human teacher. He has not left that open to us. He did not intend to."

Brother Hedrick also states that every false religion, every false religious system agrees on this one point: Jesus is not God. So this doctrine, more than any other, is the dividing line between orthodoxy and heresy (truth and error).

C.S. Lewis said:

> "A man who was merely a man and said the sort of things Jesus said would not be a great moral teacher. He would either be a lunatic - on the level with a man who says he is a poached egg - or else he would be the devil of hell" - *(Messianic Perspectives*, p. 4, January-February 2005).[1]

---

[1] NOTE: This is a notable statement coming from C. S. Lewis who himself was erroneous on many Bible doctrines; but here, he has the good sense to allude to Christ's Deity. According to an article in The Perilous Times, pp 1, 5, Jan/Feb, 2006, C. S Lewis, the distinguished professor of English literature

Either Jesus was and IS God in the flesh or else a madman or something worse.

Of course, many good Catholics, as well as some Protestants and Baptists that are not saved, believe mentally that Jesus is God. Actually, lost sinners coming to God for salvation, must believe that **Jesus is God - John 8:24**.)

Saving faith must come from the heart (**Romans 10:9-10**).

Jesus Claimed to be Equal With God the Father and Accepted Worship From Men:

> *John 5:18:* "Therefore the Jews sought the more to kill him, because he not only had broken the Sabbath, but said also that God was his Father **making himself equal with God**,"
> *John 5:23:* "That all men **should honour the Son, even as they honour the Father**. He that honoureth not the Son honoureth not the Father which hath sent him."
> *John 5:22:* "For the Father judgeth no man, but hath committed all judgment unto the Son."
> *John 8:56-58:* "Your father Abraham rejoiced to see my day: and he saw it, and was glad. Then said the Jews unto him, thou art not yet fifty years old, and hast thou seen Abraham? Jesus said unto them, Verily, verily, I say unto you, **Before Abraham was, I am.**

---

at Cambridge University--went to a priest for regular confession—prayed for the dead—held strongly to an evolutionary animal ancestry of man—held that the Genesis account came from pagan mythical sources—did not believe in a bodily resurrection—said the Book of Job is "unhistorical"—said the Bible contained "error"—that the Bible "carries" the Word of God and is "human material" - believed that salvation was a process - evolution was correct—that purgatory in the after-life is required—that Christianity owes much to paganism—that God can be found through other heathen religions—says hell is not a place God sends people who disbelieve the gospel, but a state of mind one chooses to possess and become… Of course, many good Catholics, as well as some Protestants and Baptists that are not saved, believe mentally that Jesus is God. Actually, lost sinners coming to God for salvation, must believe that **Jesus is God - John 8:24**.

John 10:30: I and my Father are one."
John 10:33: *"The Jews answered him, saying, For a good work we stone thee not; but for blasphemy; and because that **thou, being a man, makest thyself God**."*
John 14:6: *"Jesus saith unto him, **I am the way, the truth, and the life:** no man cometh unto the Father, but by me."*
John 14:8-9: "Philip saith unto him, Lord, shew us the Father, and it sufficeth us. Jesus saith unto him, Have I been so long time with you, and yet hast thou not known me, Philip? He that hath seen me hath seen the Father; and how sayest thou then, Shew us the Father?"
John 20:28: *"And Thomas answered and said unto him (Jesus), **My Lord and my God**."*
See Matthew *2:11; 11:27;* **John** *6:46; 9:38.*

"Unfallen" angels refused to be worshipped by men! The chief "fallen" angel, Satan, desires to be worshipped by men.

Israel's Unbelief Gave Them No Rest

Hebrews 4:8: *"For if Jesus had given them rest, then would he not afterward have spoken of another day. There remaineth therefore a rest to the people of God."*

In reference to the hardness of heart of OT Israel in Hebrews 3:1-19; 4:1-10, God and Jesus are synonymous as one and the same in the matter of giving rest or not giving rest to the people of God. Since the writing of the book of Hebrews, Jews and Gentiles are admonished not to harden their hearts as in the provocation of Israel in the day of temptation in the wilderness. **Jesus is God.**

How Did Old Testament Sacrifices Affect Sin?

The sacrifices offered in the Old Testament did not take away sin - (**Hebrews** 10:4; **Hebrews** 9:11-16, 23-24); they were temporary coverings (atonements) to hold off the judgment of God against sin until the perfect sacrifice would be offered - (**Hebrews** 9:28; **Galatians** 4:4) once and forever.

If OT law could save no one (**Galatians** 2:16; 3:21), it is certain that no works of any contemporary religion can offer salvation in their sacraments, works, education, or church authority. The law is holy and righteous but it did not save; it condemned those (all) who could not keep it.

Galatians 3:10-11, 13: For as many as are of the works of the law are under the curse: for it is written, Cursed is every one that continueth not in all things which are written in the book of the law to do them. But that **no man is justified by the law in the sight of God**, it is evident: for, the just shall live by faith. Christ hath redeemed us from the curse of the law, being made a curse for us: for it is written, Cursed is every one that hangeth on a tree.

The Apostle Paul Proposed an Obvious Question Pertaining to the Purpose of the Mosaic Law:

Galatians 3:19, 21-24: "Wherefore then serveth the law? It was added because of transgressions, till the seed (promised Messiah) should come to whom the promise was made; and it was ordained by angels in the hand of a mediator. Is the law then against the promises of God? God forbid: for if there had been a law given which could have given life, verily righteousness should have been by the law. But the scripture hath concluded all under sin, that the promise by faith of Jesus Christ might be given to them that believe. But before faith came, we were kept under the law, shut up unto the faith which should afterwards be revealed. The law was our schoolmaster to bring us unto Christ, that we might be justified by faith."

No one can be justified (declared righteous) before God except they come through His beloved Son, Jesus - (John 14:6). -See **Galatians** 2:16, 21; 3:10-14, 19-23; 4:4, 5; 5:3-6; **Romans** 3:20, 28; 4:4-6, 13-16; 5:1; 6:14; **Ephesians** 2:8-9; Titus 3:4.

If Jesus is Not God, an Imperfect Sacrifice For Sin Was Offered and

No One is Saved:

Hebrews 10:4: *For it is not possible that the blood of bulls and of goats should take away sins.*

Also see **Romans** 3:24, 28; 4:6; 5:8-9; 7:4, 7; **Galatians** 2:16; 21; 3:10, 13, 19; 4:4; **Hebrews** 1:3; 7:19, 22, 27; 9:14, 26, 28; 10:4, 10, 12, 14.

Jesus' blood does not just cover sin, it cleanses from all sin (**Revelation** 1:5; **I John** 1:7). If Jesus is not God, His blood could not be efficacious (accomplish the desired effect; having the intended result for sin).

At a future Time, Every Man and Angel Will Bow the Knee Before Jesus Christ and Every Tongue Will Confess That Jesus Christ is Lord

Philippians 2:9-11: *"Wherefore God also hath highly exalted him, and given him a name which is above every name: That at the name of Jesus every knee should bow, of things in heaven, and things in earth, and things under the earth; And that every tongue* *should confess that Jesus Christ is Lord, to the glory of God the Father."*

No mere man is worthy to be worshipped by angels, prophets, apostles, kings, and great men. Only Jesus, the God-man is worthy of this great honor of His Father.

If Jesus is not God come in the flesh, many Scriptures would be contradicted. Too, every true Christian would be guilty of great error and **idolatry** as well.

> **Hebrews 1:8-9:** *"But unto the Son he (God the Father) saith, Thy throne, O God (God the Son), is for ever and ever: a scepter of righteousness is the scepter of thy kingdom. Thou has loved righteousness, and hated iniquity; therefore God, even thy God, hath anointed thee with the oil of gladness above thy fellows."*

Of course, the context is of God the Father addressing His Son Jesus as God.

The practice of Open and Public Worship of Idols in Many False Religions Today Usurp the Glory Due to God:

> **Exodus 20:3-5:** *"Thou shalt have no other gods before me. Thou shalt not make unto thee **any graven image**, or **any likeness of any thing** that is in heaven above, or that is in the earth beneath, or that is in the water under the earth: Thou **shalt not bow down thyself to them,** nor serve them: for I the LORD thy God am a jealous God, visiting the iniquity of the fathers upon the children unto the third ad fourth generation of them that hate me."*

Those that worship God must worship Him directly in Spirit and truth, not through objects; points of contact, or mediums such as statues, relics, crosses, icons, images, etc.

John 4:24: "God is a Spirit: and they that worship him must worship him in spirit and truth."

CHAPTER 3

FACTS ABOUT JESUS

Jesus Saves
GOD is the Only Saviour:

a.) Jesus Is The Saviour: Matthew 1:21; Luke 2:11; John 1:12; 4:41, 42; 10:9; 14:6; Acts 4:12; 4:10; I Corinthians 3:11; Philippians 3:20; I Timothy 1:1, 15; **2 Timothy** 1:10; **Titus** 1:4; 2:13; 3:6; **2 Peter** 1:1, 11; 2:20; 3:18; **I John** 3:16; 4:14; 5:11, 12.

Those who reject the deity of Jesus have no Saviour.

b.) God Is The Saviour: **Isaiah** 43:11; 45:15; 60:16; **I Timothy** 1:1; 2:3; 4: 10; **Titus** 1:3, 4; 3:4; **Jude** 25. Cf. **Titus** 3:6. **Luke** 1:47 Cf. **Luke** 2:11. -Cf. **Hosea** 13:4; **Psalms** 18:2; 62:2, 6, 7; 78:35; **Deuteronomy** 32:4, 15, 18; **2 Samuel** 22:32; 23:3; **Matthew** 16:16, 18; **Romans** 9:33; **I Corinthians** 10:4; **I Peter** 2:6-8; **Ephesians** 4:5.

Jesus is Messias Christ:

See **Matthew** 1:16; 16:16, 20; **Mark** 14:61-64; **Luke** 2:11, 26; 4:41; 9:20; 24:26; **John** 1:41; 4:25, 26, 42; 20:31; **Acts** 2:36; **Romans** 5:21; 6:23; **I Corinthians** 5:7; **Revelation** 20:6.

Jesus is Creator:

See **John** 1:3, 10; **Ephesians** 3:9; **Hebrews** 1:8-12; **Colossians** 1:12-17; **I Corinthians** 8:6; **Revelation** 4:8-11; 10:6; 14:6-7; 21:5-7; 22:3; **Isaiah** 40.

Jesus is the great "I AM."

See **Mark** 14:62; **John** 8:24-28; 18:5-8; **Revelation** 1:17-18. **See also John** 6:48, 51; 7:28, 29; 8:12, 24, 28, 58; 9:5; 10:7, 9-10, 11, 14, 36; 11:23, 25; 13:3, 19; 14:6; 18:5-6, 8; **Revelation** 22:13, 16.

- -Mark 14:62---Jesus said, **I AM** (the Christ, the Son of the Blessed)
- -John 6:35---**I AM** the Bread of Life
- -John 6:51---**I AM** the Living Bread which came down from heaven
- -John 7:29---**I AM** from Him
- -John 8:12; 9:5---**I AM** the Light of the World
- -John 8:23---**I AM** from above
- -John 8:24, 28---**I AM** (He)
- -John 9:9---**I AM** (He)
- -John 8:58---Before Abraham was, **I AM**
- -John 10:7---**I AM** the Door of the Sheep
- -John 10:9---**I AM** the Door (to the Father and to salvation)
- -John 10:11, 14---**I AM** the Good Shepherd
- -John 10:36---**I AM** the Son of God
- -John 11:25---**I AM** the Resurrection and the Life
- -John 13:13---**I AM** (Lord and Master)
- -John 13:19---**I AM** (He)
- -John 14:6---**I AM** the Way; the Truth, and the Life
- -John 14:10---**I AM** in the Father
- -John 15:1---**I AM** the True Vine
- -John 15:5---**I AM** the Vine

- -John 17:14---**I AM** not of the world
- -John 18:5, 6, 8---**I AM** (He)
- -Revelation 1:8---**I AM** Alpha (A) and Omega (Ω), the Beginning and the Ending
- -Revelation 1:11---**I AM** Alpha and Omega, the First and the Last
- -Revelation 1:17---**I AM** the First and the Last
- -Revelation 1:18---**I AM** alive for evermore
- -Revelation 21:6---**I AM** Alpha and Omega, the Beginning and the End
- -Revelation 22:13---**I AM** Alpha and Omega, the Beginning and the End, the First and the Last
- -Revelation 22:16---**I AM** the Root and the Offspring of David, and the Bright and Morning Star

It would be no less than blasphemy for a mere mortal man and nothing less than Deity to make these divine claims.

In The OT, JEHOVAH God referred to Himself as "I AM."

Exodus 3:14: "And God said unto Moses, I AM THAT I AM: and he said, Thus shalt thou say unto the children of Israel, I AM hath sent me unto you."

In the NT, JESUS expressly claimed to be The Great **"I AM"** Who was before Abraham's time.

John 8:58: "Jesus said unto them (unbelieving Jews), Verily, verily, I say unto you, **Before Abraham was, I AM**."

A Christian brother (**Henry M. Morris**) wrote that it is very interesting to note the frequency of "I AM" claims in the Bible. They occur in multiples of seven:

- There are seven "I am"s in the Book of Genesis

- There are 21 (i.e., 3 x 7) "I am's" in the Book of Exodus
- The Book of Psalms contains seven "I am's" that speak prophetically (future sufferings of the incarnate Christ) – **Psalms** 22:6; 40:17; 69:8; 69:20; 69:29; 102:7; 102:11.
- The second division of Isaiah (Isaiah 40-66) contains 35 claims (7x5). However, the first division of Isaiah, which has a different theme than the second division that emphasizes prophecy, has not such "I am" statements.
- The Book of Ezekiel contains 70 of these great assertions (more than any other single book).
- Jeremiah contains 21 of these statements.
- Then, all of the smaller prophetical books of the prophets have a total of 21 "I am's."
- All told, the 17 prophetical books contain a total of 154 (22x7) of God's great "I am" claims.
- The Gospel of John contains seven of the most beautiful of the "I am's:"
    - "I am the bread of life" – John 6:35, 48, 51
    - "I am the light of the world" – John 8:12
    - "I am the door of the sheep" – John 10:7, 9
    - "I am the good shepherd" – John 10:11, 14
    - "I am the resurrection, and the life" – John 11:25
    - "I am the way, the truth, and the life" – John 14:6
    - "I am the true vine" – John 15:1, 5

A madman or a charlatan (seller of papal indulgences; fake) might make such a claim, but no honest person could ever do so...unless it was a true claim.

There are also seven great "I am" statements in the Book of Revelation – **Revelation** 1:8; 1:18; 1:11; 1:17; 21:6; 22:13; 22:16.

There are other "7"s in the Book of Revelation (churches, Spirits, candlesticks, stars, lamps, horns, eyes, angels, trumpets, heads, crowns, plagues, seals, thunders, mountains, kings, thousands, vials, etc.) Revelation is the book of sevens; the word "seven" occurs over fifty times. Seven is a significant biblical number in that it signifies "final" or "completion."

Jesus Claimed Deity When He Was Arrested in the Garden:

When Judas brought the band of men and officers from the chief priests and Pharisees, Jesus answered them, "I am he" - John 18:3 -8. Notice that the *he* is italicized in the KJV indicating that the word *he* was supplied by the translators and is not in the copies of the original Greek manuscripts. Therefore, Jesus said, **"I AM."** As soon as Jesus had spoken the two words "I AM," this divine declaration of His glorious essence as God forced the band of men to go backwards and fall to the ground – (**John 18:6**).

Again, compare this with Jehovah God in the OT:

Exodus 3:14: *"And God said unto Moses, I AM THAT I AM: and he said, Thus shalt thou say unto the children of Israel, I AM hath sent me unto you."*

Jesus is the First and Last:

See-Revelation 1:17; 22:13 cf. Isaiah 44:6. Colossians 1:17 cf. Genesis 1:1.

Jesus is Lord:

See **Malachi** 3:1 cf. **Matthew** 11:7-10.

I Timothy 6:15-16: *"Which in his times he shall shew, who is **the blessed and only Potentate**, the King of kings, and Lord of lords; Who only hath immortality, dwelling in the light which no man can approach unto; who no man hath seen, nor can see: to whom be honour and power everlasting. Amen."*

Neither vain preacher, pompous pope, cardinal, archbishop, rabbi, monk, imam, or guru is **Potentate**.

Jesus is called "LORD" 663 times in the New Testament. The Greek word "Kurios" is the equivalent of the Hebrew "Adonai" and is so used by Jesus in **Matthew 22:43-45**.

However, kurios (master) is used also of mere human relationships- (**Mathew** 6:24; 15:27; **Mark** 13:35; **Ephesians** 6:9).

> **Acts 9:17:** *"Ananias went his way, and entered into the house; and putting his hands on him said, Brother Saul, **the Lord, even Jesus**, that appeared unto thee in the way as thou camest, hath sent me, that thou mightest receive thy sight, and be filled with the Holy Ghost."*

In this verse, Ananias clearly identified "the Lord" and Jesus as one and the same person.

Again, the word translated *"lord"* is sometimes used in the New Testament in speaking of men (**Acts** 25:26), but not in the same way that it is used of Christ. Jesus is spoken of as *"The Lord"* just as Jehovah God is spoken of as The Lord.

> **Acts 4:26, 33:** *"The kings of the earth stood up, and the rulers were gathered together against **The Lord, and against his Christ**. And with great power gave the apostles witness of the resurrection of The Lord Jesus: and great grace was upon them all.*
> **Psalms 2:2-3:** *"The kings of the earth set themselves, and the rulers take counsel together, against **the Lord, and against his Anointed**, saying, Let us break their bands asunder, and cast away their cords from us."*

The intent to identify Jesus Christ with the OT Deity is evident from **Matthew** 3:3; 12:8; 21:9; **Psalms** 118:26; 22:43-45; **Luke** 1:43; **John** 8:58; 14:8-10; 20:28; **Acts** 9:5; 13:33; **Psalms** 2.

Jesus is God:

See **Matthew** *1:23; 16:16; 22:44-45;* **Mark** *2:10; 4:41; 14:61-62;* **Luke** *2:11; 9:20; 22:67-71;* **John** *1:1-3, 14; 4:25; 10:24-25, 28, 30; 11:27; 14:9; 17:1-5; 18:5-8; 19:7; 20:28, 31;* **Acts** *7:59; 8:37;* **I Corinthians** *8:6;* **Ephesians** *4:6;* **Philippians** *2:6;* **Colossians** *1:13-18;* **I Timothy** *2:5; 4:10; 6:14-15;* **Titus** *2:13;* **Hebrews** *1:8;* **-cf. Psalms** *90:2;* **Isaiah** *43:10; 44:8; 45:5-6, 20-22; 46:9;* **Hosea** *11:9;* **Deuteronomy** *6:4; 4:35, 39;* **Psalms** *2:7;* **II Samuel** *7:14;* **Psalms** *104:4; 45:6-7; 102:25-27.*

Jesus' Words are Forever:

See Matthew 24:35; Luke 7:36-50; 21:33; John cf. Isaiah 49:8; Psalms 138:2; I Peter 1:25

Jesus Forgave Sin:

See **Mark** 2:1-12; **Luke** 7:48-50; **Hebrews** 1:3. No one can forgive and justify the guilt of sin except God.

Matthew 12:31-32: *"Wherefore I say unto you, All manner of sin and blasphemy shall be forgiven unto men; but blasphemy against the Holy Ghost shall not be forgiven unto men. And whosoever speaketh a word against the Son of man, it shall be forgiven him: but whosoever speaketh against the Holy Ghost, it shall not be forgiven him, neither in this world, neither in the world to come."*
John 5:22: *"For the Father judgeth no man, but hath committed all judgment unto the Son."*

Jesus Raised the Dead:

See **John** 5:28-29; 6:39-44

Of course, Jesus also empowered his apostles to raise the dead as well as to physically heal.

Jesus is Eternal:

Jesus has always existed and always will.

See Hebrews 13:8 cf. Isaiah 9:6; John 8:58. John 17:5, 24 cf. Micah 5:2

Jesus is Omnipotent:
(all-powerful)

See **Luke** 4:35-36, 39, 41; 7:14; **Matthew** 8:16, 26-27; **John** 5:25

Jesus is Omniscient:
(all-knowing)

See **John** 4:16-19; 2:24-25; **Mark** 2:8; **Luke** 5:22; **Acts** 1:24

Jesus is Omnipresent:
(everywhere present)

See **Matthew** 18:20; 28:20; **John** 13:3

Jesus is Omnificent:
(unlimited creative power)

See **Colossians** 1:16-17

Jesus is Omni-sapient:
(all wisdom)

See I Timothy 1:17; Jude 25

Jesus is Immutable:
(unchangeable)

See Hebrews 1:12; 13:8

Jesus is From Heaven:

See I Corinthians 15:47

Jesus is Without Sin:

See 2 Corinthians 5:21; Hebrews 4:15; James 1:1. John 8:46 cf. I John 3:9

Jesus is The Resurrection and the Life:

*John 11:25-26: "Jesus said unto her, **I am the resurrection, and the life**: he that believeth in me, though he were dead, yet shall he live: And whosoever liveth and believeth in me shall never die. Believest thou this?"*

"Doubting" Thomas believed in the resurrection of Jesus Christ because of proof. Thomas' confession to Jesus could not be said any better, "...My Lord and my God" - (John 20:28). Thomas was convinced beyond any doubt that Jesus is God.

The Scriptures declare Jesus to be the Son of God by the Resurrection:

Romans 1:3-4: "Concerning his Son Jesus Christ our Lord, which was made of the seed of David according *to the flesh; And declared to be the Son of God with power, according to the spirit of holiness, **by the resurrection** from the dead."*

As previously shown, the Scriptures declare the attributes of God the Son to be the same as the attributes of God the Father

- ✓ Jesus knows all things - **John** 1:48; 2:25; 6:24; 16:30; 21:17
- ✓ Jesus is eternal - **Miciah** 5:2; **John** 17:4-5; **Isaiah** 44:5; **Revelation** 1:17
- ✓ Jesus is all-powerful - **Matthew** 28:18; **Hebrews** 1:3
- ✓ Jesus is sinless - **John** 8:46
- ✓ Jesus is unchanging - **Hebrews** 13:18
- ✓ Jesus has the power to forgive sins - **Mark** 2:5-7
- ✓ Jesus controls nature - **Mattthew** 8:26
- ✓ Jesus judges the world - **John** 5:22, 27
- ✓ Jesus is worshipped by angels - **Hebrews** 1:6

The KING of ISRAEL

- ➤ **Jehovah** God is the King of Israel in the OT – (**Zephaniah 3:15**).
- ➤ **Jesus**, the Son of God, is the King of Israel in the NT – (**John 1:49; 12:13**).

God Sings and Jesus Sings:

It is no proof that Jesus is God but it is interesting to note that Jehovah God sang in the OT – (**Zephaniah 3:17**); this appears to be at a future time when Israel is to be restored during the Millennium. It also appears that Jesus sang a hymn with the disciples at the Lord's Supper - (**Matthew 26:30**).

JESUS is Called "MIGHTY GOD" and "EVERLASTING FATHER" in the OT:

*Isaiah 9:6: "For unto us **a child is born**, unto us a **son is given**: and the government shall be upon his shoulder: and **his name** shall be called Wonderful, Counsellor, **The mighty God**, **The everlasting Father**, The Prince of Peace."*

Here in the OT, two persons of the triune Godhead are one and the same, God the Father and God the Son. In the NT, they are the same - (**I John 5:7-13; Matthew 11:27; 16:16; Luke 10:22; John 1:18; 5:18, 21; 6:46; 8:19; 10:30, 38; 14:9, 11**).

JESUS is Called Both LORD (Yahweh = Jehovah) and God (Elohim) in the OT:

*Isaiah 40:3: "The voice of him (John Baptist) that crieth in the wilderness, Prepare ye the way of the **LORD** (Jehovah Jesus– Luke 3:4), make straight in the desert a highway for our God (Elohim)."*

NOTE: When **LORD** is spelled in all capital letters, it is the same as Jehovah.

Of course, this is a prophecy concerning John the Baptist's announcement of the Lamb of God, Jesus. This prophecy is easily identified in the NT. See **Matthew 3:2, 5; Luke 1:17; John 1:23, 29.**

Luke 3:3-4: "And he (John the Baptist) came into all the country about Jordan, preaching the baptism of repentance for the remission of sins; As it is written in the book of the words of Esaias the prophet, saying, The voice of one crying in the wilderness, Prepare ye the way of the Lord (Jehovah Jesus – Isaiah 40:3), make his paths straight."

Jesus is Called
Both *"great GOD"* and *"Saviour:"*

Titus 2:13: "Looking for that blessed hope, and the glorious appearing of the great God and our Saviour Jesus Christ."

The Lord of The Old Testament Was Pierced
and Jesus of The New Testament was Pierced:

Zechariah 12:10: "And I will pour upon the house of David, and upon the inhabitants of Jerusalem, the spirit of grace and of supplications: and they shall look upon **me who they have pierced**, and they shall morn for him, as one mourneth for his only son, and shall be in bitterness for him, as one that is in bitterness for his firstborn."
John 19:34: "But one of the soldiers with a spear **pierced his side**, and forthwith came there out blood and water."

In Both OT and NT Prophecies of Christ's Birth,
Jesus is Declared to be
God in the Flesh;

Isaiah 7:14: Therefore the Lord himself shall give you a sign: Behold**, a virgin** shall conceive, and bear a **Son**, and shall call his **name Immanuel.**

Immanuel means "God with us"--Matthew 1:23. This prophecy of the virgin birth of Christ was prophesied over 500 years before its fulfillment. and was announced to Joseph (foster-father of Jesus) by the angel, Gabriel - **Matthew** 1:20.

Matthew 1:23: "Behold**, a virgin** shall be with child, and shall bring forth **a son**, and they shall call his name **Emmanuel**, which being interpreted is, **God with us**."

This verse interprets itself. Jesus, the Son, is God in the flesh with us. God actually became a man, but a perfect man *"made of a woman"* - **Galatians 4:4**. *"He saith...a body hast thou prepared me"* **Hebrews 10:5**. Again, a child can read **Matthew 1:23-25** and figure out the identity of this Son! Phony religionists cannot understand plain Bible language (or they can understand and refuse to believe God's Word).

<u>Note:</u> Unbelievers do not believe in the Deity of Christ because they are of their father, the devil – (John 8:44).

The "Great Question" that every man has to answer is: **IS JESUS THE CHRIST OF GOD COME IN THE FLESH TO DIE FOR MY SINS?**

There is no avoiding this greatest question of all time. What a man answers to this question determines his eternal standing, in either Heaven or Hell.

> *I John 5:5:* "Who is he that overcometh the world, but he that believeth that **Jesus is the Son of God**."
> *I John 4:3:* "And every spirit that confesseth not that Jesus Christ is come in the flesh is not of God: and this is that spirit of antichrist, whereof ye have heard that it should come; and even now already is it in the world."
> *I John 2:22-23:* "Who is a liar, but he that denieth that Jesus is the Christ? He is antichrist, that denieth that Father and the Son. Whosoever denieth the Son, the same hath not the Father; but he that <u>acknowledgeth the Son</u> hath the Father also."
> *I John 2:18:* "Little children, it is the last time: and as ye have heard that antichrist shall come, even now are there many antichrists; whereby we know that it is the last time."

The cult religion called Jehovah Witness is well known for the denial of the Deity of Christ (as are many other cults).

What is Arianism?

"Arianism" is a doctrine of Arius (A.D. 256?--336) that declared that the Son (Jesus) is not of the same substance as the Father but was *created* as an agent for creating the world. The teaching of Arianism began about AD 318 with Arius, a priest of Alexandria, Egypt. Arius did not believe that Jesus was eternal. Even today, there are those false religions that teach that Jesus is inferior to God the Father. They deny the deity of Jesus Christ in spite of many plain statements in the Scriptures - (**Matthew** 1:23; **I Timothy** 3:16).

This false teaching (Arianism) is propagated today by "religionists" under the guise of serving Jehovah God. Jesus, as God, could not have died for sinners unless He partook of a body of flesh (**Galatians 4:4**). Jesus, as God-man had to die for sinners because there was no one else worthy to pay the supreme sacrifice (no man; no angel; no other entity) that was required by God to expiate[2] sin. **Anything created (Arianism), whether angel or superior being, could not propitiate∗ sin.**

Salvation is not in having a comfortable religion; it is Christ in you (**Colossians 1:27**) and what He did for us - (**Acts** 3:20; **Romans** 4:25; **I Corinthians** 15:3-4; **I Corinthians** 15:17; **2 Corinthians** 5:17; **Colossians** 1:22-24; 2:11-12).

The Prophetic Time of the Church Age Has Nearly Run Its Course.

It is time to awake!

Romans 13:11-12: "And that, knowing the time, that now it is high time to awake out of sleep: for now is our salvation nearer than when we believed. ***The night is far spent, the day is at hand****: let us therefore cast off*

---

[2] **Expiate** = put an end to; make amends for; extinguish the guilt incurred by

the works of darkness, and let us put on the armour of light."

Think of how much nearer is the day approaching than when nearly two-thousand years ago the apostle Paul wrote this. That "spirit of antichrist" is stronger today than ever before because we are nearing the beginning of the 70th Week of Daniel spoken of in Daniel's Seventy Weeks of prophecy (Daniel 9:24-27). Daniel's 70th Week is the Tribulation Period (7-years) and the last week determined upon the Jews (Daniel 9:27). This horrible time of judgment upon earth is described in the Book of Revelation, chapters 6-19. The last 3½ years of the Seventh-Week (one week = 7 years) is the closest thing to Hell upon earth that one could imagine. Before this time of *"Jacob's Trouble"* (Jeremiah 30:7) begins, the First Resurrection (the main body of believers) will occur. This resurrection (many call it the "rapture") will be the raising of the dead saints first and then the translation of live saints. The dead in Christ and the living in Christ will all be caught up together in resurrection bodies in clouds (I Thessalonians 4:16-17) to meet the Lord in the air. There are many antichrist spirits that deny that Christ is come in the flesh and that He will come for His church, the Bride of Christ.

> *I John 4:2-3:* *"Hereby know ye the Spirit of God: Every spirit that confesseth that Jesus Christ is come in the flesh is of God: And every spirit that confesseth not that Jesus Christ is come in the flesh is not of God: and this is that spirit of antichrist, whereof ye have heard that it should come; and even now already is it in the world."*

Christ *"is come in the flesh."* Anyone that denies the Deity of Jesus Christ, and that He has come and taken on the body of a man *"is not of God"* but rather is of "that spirit of antichrist" (**I John 2:22-23; 2 John 7-10**). There are many false prophets (New Age teachers, liberal religionists, rabbis, gurus, and mullahs) that deny that Jesus is the Christ.

Jesus Christ (being both God and man at the same time) died for our sins and rose again, which was a physical death and bodily resurrection.

Jesus said to the unbelieving Jewish religionists:

> *"Search the scriptures; for in them ye think ye have eternal life: and they are they which testify of me. For had ye believed Moses, ye would have believed me: for he wrote of me. But if ye believe not his writings, how shall ye believe my words?" - (**John 5:39, 46-47**)*

The unbelieving Jews did not acknowledge the fulfillment of the Old Testament writings of Moses (OT Scriptures) concerning the Messiah. Jesus tells them that He Himself is the Messiah promised by Moses' writings.

> ***John 8:19, 23-24:*** *"Then said they unto him, Where is thy Father? Jesus answered, Ye neither know me, nor my Father: if ye had known me, ye should have known my Father also. And he said unto them, Ye are from beneath; I am from above: ye are of the world; I am not of this world. I said therefore unto you, **that ye shall die in your sins: for if ye believe not that I am he, ye shall die in your sins.**"*

Scriptures plainly teach that those who reject Christ as Messiah are of the spirit of antichrist.

Jesus is Eternal (always been):

Jesus did not begin to exist upon His birth in a body of flesh. He is in **the bosom** of the Father -

> **John 1:18:** *"No man hath seen God at any time; the only Begotten Son, which is in the bosom of the Father, he hath declared him."*

Jesus preexisted before His incarnation into a body of flesh. God hath declared Him, and He is God's only begotten Son whose goings forth have been from of old, from everlasting - (**John** 1:1-3; 3:16; **Colossians** 1:16).

> **Micah 5:2:** *"But thou, Beth-lehem Ephratah, though thou be little among the thousands of Judah, yet out of thee shall he (Jesus) come forth unto me that is to be ruler in Israel; whose goings forth have been from of old, **from everlasting**."*

God of the OT is *the First and the Last* - (**I Samuel** 41:4; **Isaiah 44:6; 48:12**).

Jesus of the NT is *the First and the Last* - (**Revelation 1:11, 17; 2:8; 22:13**).

If Jesus is not God, He could not have been the First and the Last! Actually, it would be blasphemy for anyone less than God to make this claim. The *"First and Last"* is equivalent to *"The Beginning and the Ending,"* and *"I am Alpha and Omega"* - (**Revelation 1:8, 11, 17; 21:6; 22:13**). Of course, alpha **(A)** and omega **(Ω)** are the first and last letters of the Greek alphabet. This denotes the supremacy and sovereignty of God and that all things have a beginning and ending with God. There is nothing in between. Again, there is only one *"First and Last."* Jesus, being God in the flesh, says that He is the First and Last which **was dead** (as the sacrificial offering to God for man's sin), and is alive (resurrection power).

> *Revelation 2:8: "And unto the angel of the church in Smyrna write; These things saith the first and the last, which was dead, and is alive."*

It doesn't take a deep theologian to understand this Scripture. Many children know that **Jesus is The First and Last** who died on a cross for sinners and resurrected the third day. We are told who this person is in Revelation 1:11, 17-20.

> *Revelation 1:5, 8: "And from Jesus Christ, who is the faithful witness, and the first begotten of the dead, and the prince of the kings of the earth. Unto him that loved us, and washed us from our sins in his own blood. I am Alpha and Omega, the beginning and the ending, saith the Lord, which is and which was, and which is to come, the Almighty."*

It is expressly stated that Jesus is the Almighty and The Beginning and The Ending. What part do the slow-witted false religionists not understand? Perhaps they need to return to grade school to learn again basic definitions.

- Jesus is the first to resurrect in a *glorified* body (first begotten of the dead)
- Jesus is the prince of the kings of the earth
- Jesus washed us from our sins in His own blood (Revelation 1:5)
- Jesus is Alpha and Omega, The Beginning and the Ending
- Jesus was dead, and is alive (**Revelation 2:8**)
- Jesus is the Almighty

As Stated Before, God the Father Calls His Son, *"O God"*:

> *Hebrews 1:8: "But unto the Son (Jesus) he (God the Father) saith, Thy throne (Jesus' throne), O God, is for ever and ever: a sceptre of righteousness is the sceptre of thy kingdom."*

Psalms 110:1: *"The Lord (Jehovah) said unto my Lord (Jesus), Sit thou at my right hand, until I make thine enemies thy footstool."*

Again, Jesus is Declared to be the Son of God by the Resurrection:

Romans 1:3-4: *"Concerning his Son Jesus Christ our Lord, which was made of the seed of David according to the flesh; And declared to be the Son of God with power, according to the spirit of holiness, by the resurrection from the dead."*

Jesus Calls Himself LORD in the OT:

Zechariah 3:2: *"And the LORD (**God The Son**) said unto Satan, The LORD (**God The Father**; Jehovah) rebuke thee, O Satan; even the LORD (Jehovah) that hath chosen Jerusalem rebuke thee: is not this a brand plucked out of the fire?"*

Jesus Appeared in the OT Before His Incarnation in the Likeness of Men (Philippians 2:7):

Jesus in Old Testament in pre-incarnate forms: **Genesis** 16:1-13; 21:17-19; 22:11-16; 31:11-13; **Exodus** 3:2-4; **Judges** 2:1; 6:12-16; 13:3-22.

Again, these pre-incarnate Old Testaments manifestations of Jesus are commonly referred to as "Theophanies" or "Christophanies."

The writer believes that the fourth man in the burning fiery furnace with Shadrach, Meshach, and Abednego was none other than Jesus Christ, God's Darling Son, in a pre-incarnate form - (**Daniel 3:16-26**).

One of the three men to visit Abraham in Genesis 18 was Jesus manifested in pre-incarnate form - (**Genesis 18:1, 13, 22, 33**). The other two, who appeared as men, were angels sent to destroy Sodom - (**Genesis** 18:16; 19:1, 13).

Jesus is the "Only Way" of salvation:

See **John** 6:29, 35, 40, 47; 14:6, 9; **Acts** 4:12; **I Timothy** 2:5:

I John 5:1: "Whosoever believeth that Jesus is the Christ is born of God: and every one that loveth him that begat loveth him also that is begotten of him."
*II John 7-9: "For **many deceivers** are entered into the world, **who confess not that Jesus Christ is come in the flesh.** This is a deceiver and an antichrist. Look to yourselves, that we lose not those things which we have wrought, but that we receive a full reward. Whosoever transgresseth, and abideth not in the doctrine of Christ, hath not God. He that abideth in the doctrine of Christ, he hath both the Father and the Son."*
I John 4:6: "We are of God: he that knoweth God heareth us; he that is not of God heareth not us. Hereby know we the Spirit of truth, and the spirit of error."
Proverbs 14:12; 16:25: "There is a way which seemeth right unto a man, but the end thereof are the ways of death."

No Denomination or Sect Can Claim a Private Way of Salvation

The only way to Heaven is the Bible way. There is not a Baptist way, a Methodist way, a Presbyterian way, a Pentecostal way, and a Catholic way. The Bible way is, JESUS IS THE ONLY WAY TO HEAVEN - (**John 14:6; I Timothy 2:5**). Neither can a Scripture text be removed from its context in order to prove a private doctrine.

Someone has stated, "A text without a context is a pretext."

This rules out the works of man such as: good works; human merit; baptism; communion; ordinances; sacraments;

confessionals; tradition, church affiliation; denominational sanctioning; doing good; education, etc.

For proof texts, see **Ephesians** 2:8-10; **Romans** 4:4-6; **Galatians** 2:16: **Romans** 3:10, 23; 10:9-17; **John** 14:6; **Acts** 4:12; **I Timothy** 2:5; **John** 3:3, 5, 7, 16.

Nature Obeys Jesus:

Mark 4:41: And they feared exceedingly, and said one to another, What manner of man is this, that even the <u>wind</u> and the <u>sea</u> obey him?" See Mark 4:35-41.

Jesus Knows the Heart and Mind of Man

In the New Testament...

John 2:24-25: "But Jesus did not commit himself unto them, because he knew all men, And needed not that any should testify of man: for he knew what was in man."
John 1:1: There are only three who know the innermost of man (the Father, the Word, and the Holy Ghost: and these three are one). Of course, Jesus Christ is the Word.

See Hebrews 4:12.

In the Old Testament...

*2 Chronicles 6:30: "Then hear thou (LORD God) from heaven thy dwelling place, and forgive, and render unto every man according unto all his ways, whose heart thou knowest; (for **thou only knowest the hearts of the children of men**:)"*

"And grieve not the holy Spirit of God, whereby ye are sealed unto the day of redemption."

Ephesians 4:30

CHAPTER 4

TITLES OF GOD

ASCRIBED TO JESUS

TITLES OF GOD ASCRIBED TO JESUS		
TITLE	**GOD**	**JESUS**
As Creator	**Gen.** 1:1; 2:7; Job 33:4 **Psa.** 33:6; 104:30; **Isa.** 40:28; **Isa.** 44:24; 45:11-18: **Mal.** 2:10	**John** 1:10; **Eph.** 3:9; **I Cor.** 8:6
As the **Shepherd**	**Psa.** 23; 100; **Isa.** 40:10-11	**John** 10:8-12; **Heb.** 13:20; **I Pet.** 2:21-25; 5:4
As "**I AM**"	**Ex.** 3:13-14; **Isa.** 43:10-13, 25	**John** 8:24-28; 18:5- **Rev.** 1:17,18
As the "**First and Last**	**Isa.** 41:4; 43:10,11; 44:6-8	**Rev.** 1:17; 22:13
Jesus the **King of Kings**	**Psa.** 24; 44:4; 74:12; 95:3; **Isa.** 43:10-15; 44:6-8; **Jer.** 10:10; **Zech.** 14:9	**Matt.** 2:1-6; **Luke** 19:32-38; **Luke** 23:3; **John** 19:21; **I Tim.** 6:13-16; **Rev.** 15:1-4; **Rev.** 19:11-16
Raiser of Jesus	**Acts** 10:40; 22:24	**Matt.** 26:21; **Mk.** 14:58;

		John 2:19-22
Mighty God	**Isa.** 10:21; **Jer.** 32:18	**Isa.** 9:6; **Tit.** 2:13
Only Savior	**Isa.** 43:11	**II Tim.** 1:10
Judge	**Isa.** 24:20-21	**Col.** 1:1
Reigning	**Isa.** 24:23	**Matt.** 25:31
Every Knee Bow	**Isa.** 45:23	**Phil.** 2:10-11
Alpha and Omega	**Isa.** 44:6	**Rev.** 1:7-18
Stone of Stumbling	**Isa.** 8:13-15	**I Pet.** 2:6-8

Jesus Warned the Unbelieving Religious Leaders (Pharisees) of Their Danger in Rejecting Him:

John 8:24: "I said therefore unto you, that ye shall die in your sins: for if ye believe not that I am he, ye shall die in your sins."

Again, even doubting Thomas came to the full realization that Jesus was God after Jesus' resurrection proved it to him.

*John 20:28-29: "And Thomas answered and said unto him, **My Lord and my God**. Jesus saith unto him, Thomas because thou hast seen me, thou hast believed: blessed are they that have not seen me, and yet have believed."*

It is Impossible For a Person to be Saved If They Do Not Believe That Jesus is God:

John 5:38-43: "And ye have not his (God) word abiding in you: for whom he (God) hath sent, him (Jesus) ye believe not. Search the Scriptures; for in *them ye think ye have eternal life; and they are they which testify of me (Jesus). And ye **will not** come to me (Jesus), that ye might have life. I (Jesus) receive not honour from men. But I know you, that **ye have not the love of God in you**. I (Jesus) am come in my Father's name, and ye receive me (Jesus) not; if another shall come in his own name, him (antichrist) ye will receive."*

God and His Son are One and the Same

(just as a person's soul, body, and spirit are one and the same – I Thessalonians 5:23):

> *John 14:8:* "Philip saith unto him (JESUS), Lord, shew us the Father, and it sufficeth us."
> *John 14:9:* "Jesus saith unto him, Have I been so long time with you, and yet hast thou not known me, Philip? he that hath seen me hath seen the Father, and how sayest thou then, Shew us the Father?"
> *John 10:30:* "I and my Father are one."

In truth, the highest angel in Heaven cannot claim to be one with the Father!

Lucifer desired to exalt his throne above the stars of God and be like the Most High: but Satan (Lucifer's name after his fall) was cast out of Heaven and eventually will be brought down to Hell, to the sides of the pit - (**Isaiah 14:12-15**).

Jesus is of the <u>triune</u> Godhead, God the Father, God the Son, and God the Holy Ghost.

(<u>triune</u> = "three-one." Tri = 3; une = "1.")

Perhaps it is not so much "three <u>in</u> one" but "these three are one" (**I John 5:7**).

God is three, but He is "one" God - (**Matthew** 12:28; 28:19; **Luke** 4:18-19; **John** 5:43; 6:46: 10:30; 14:10; **Isaiah** 9:6).

Earthly mathematics demand that "1+1+1 = 3," but God is not limited to natural laws. Divine mathematics is on a higher plane. *Perhaps* it is better to say "1 x 1 x 1 = 3."

The Triune Godhead is Expressed Many Times in Scriptures:

Romans 8:9: "*But ye are not in the flesh, but in the Spirit, if so be that the Spirit of God dwell in you. Now if any man have not the Spirit of Christ, he is none or his.*"

The Holy Spirit is called both the Spirit of God and the Spirit of Christ. Christ is God and so is the Holy Spirit God (pneumatology).

Baptism was to be done in the name of the Father, the Son, and the Holy Ghost (**Matthew** 28:19). God does not share His glory with none other than Himself. The three in one (**I John** 5:7) are co-equal as one.

Many Times in Scriptures, the Plural Pronoun Expresses the Trinity of the Godhead:

When God said, "Let **us** make man in **our** image, after **our** likeness..." (**Genesis** 1:26), He was not speaking of sharing His glory with angels or any other entity.

Genesis 3:22: "*And the LORD God said, Behold, the man is become as one of **us**, to know good and evil....*"
Genesis 11:7: "*Go to, let **us** go down, and there confound their language, that they may not understand one another's speech.*"
Isaiah 6:8: "*Also I heard the voice of the Lord, saying, Whom shall I send, and who will go for **us**? Then said I, Here am I; send me.*"

Song of Solomon 1:11: "**We** will make thee (the Bride) borders of gold with studs of silver."

Made in the Image of God (though the image has been marred with sin), Man Himself is Three, but One: Body, Soul, and Spirit

I Thessalonians 5:23: "And the very God of peace sanctify you wholly; and I pray God your whole **spirit** and **soul** and **body** be preserved blameless unto the coming of our Lord Jesus Christ."

It is absolutely absurd to assume that the Creator is less complex than His creation (creature) who Himself is a trinity.

How Many Ways are There to Heaven?

Most religious denominations and sects teach a "works" salvation. They teach works to obtain salvation and works to keep it. Others teach salvation as a gift of the grace of God but teach one form or another of works to retain or keep salvation. Several religions teach sacramental salvation (observing ordinances to obtain and retain salvation). One major religion teaches that the Bible is not the sole authority but that its church tradition, ordinances, and rituals have equal authority in obtaining salvation (beginning with infant baptism). All of these religions are wrong in their doctrines. There are not many ways nor many roads to Heaven.

There is Only "One Way" to Heaven:

- *John 1:12:* "But as many as received him.."
- *John 14:6:* "Jesus saith unto him, I AM the Way, the Truth, and the Life."
- *Acts 4:12:* "neither is there salvation in any other; for there is none other name..."

- *Ephesians 4:5:* "One Lord, one faith..."
- *I Timothy 2:5:* "For there is one God, and one mediator between God and men, the man Christ Jesus. (The blessed Mary and deluded earthly priests are excluded.)"
- *I John 5:11:* "...God hath given to us eternal life, and this life is in his Son."
- *John 3:36:* "He that believeth on the Son hath everlasting life: and he that believeth not the Son shall not see life; but the wrath of God abideth on him."

There are many roads leading to Rome and many ways to get to New York City, but there is only one way to Heaven, Jesus Christ. He Is God.

To the Religious "Natural Man," There is a Way That Seems Right in His Own Eyes:

Proverbs 14:12; 16:25: "There is a way which seemeth right unto a man, but the end thereof are the ways of death."
I Corinthians 2:12-14: "Now we have received, not the spirit of the world, but the spirit which is of God; that we might know the things that are freely given to us of God. Which things also we speak, not in the words which man's wisdom teacheth, but which the Holy Ghost teacheth; comparing spiritual things with spiritual. But the natural man receiveth not the things of the Spirit of God: for they are foolishness unto him: neither can he know them, because they are spiritually discerned."
John 20:30-31: "And many other signs truly did Jesus in the presence of his disciples, which are not written in this book: But these are written that ye might believe that **Jesus is the Christ, the Son of God**; and that believing ye might have life through his name."

In context, both John and Paul tell us of the signs performed by Jesus to the unbelieving Jews that they might believe and be saved

(I Corinthians 14:22). These signs were to authenticate His Gospel and His authority as the Son of God:

Jesus is Able to Save Them to the Uttermost That Come unto God by Him - (Hebrews 7:25):

To the	Jesus is
Lost	Saviour (if received as Lord)
Saved	Lord
Builder	Architect
Soldier	Captain
Nation	Sovereign
Artist	Perfect Painting
Geologist	Rock
Astronomer	Star
Anatomist	Head
Botanist	rose
Zoologist	Lamb
Lonely	Companion
Sinner	Reconciliaation
Defenseless	Fortress
Weak	Strength

-Jesus is the "Door to Heaven" - (**John 10:7, 9**)

-Jesus is the "Light of the World" - (**John 8:12**)

-Jesus is the "Bread of Life" - (**John 6:48, 51**)

-Jesus is the "True Vine" - (**John 15:1, 5**)

-Jesus is the "Living Water" - (**John 7:38-39**)

-Jesus is the "Saviour of the World" - (**John 4:42**)

JESUS IS GOD.

It is very interesting to note the Hebrew word "Salvation" In **Isaiah 12:2** (and other OT texts):

> *Isaiah 12:2: "Behold, God is my salvation; I will trust, and not be afraid: for the LORD JEHOVAH is my strength and my song; he also is become my salvation."*

"Salvation" in Hebrew is actually yeshua, or the equivalent of "Jesus" (Strong's H3444, yeshua (yesh-oo'-aw). This sentence could be read: **"He also is become my Jesus."** The Lord Jehovah, in that day, would also be the man, Jesus. Yeshua, or salvation, means something saved; victory; prosperity; deliverance; help; salvation.

Another equivalent version of the word Jesus in the OT is "Joshua," (Strong's H3091 "yhoshua" [yeh-ho-shoo'-ah]. Joshua was the Jewish leader of Israel and a type of The Captain of our Salvation, The Lord Jesus Christ.

All Men on Earth Must One Day Honor Jesus Even as They Honor the Father:

> *John 5:23: That all men should honour the Son, even as they honour the Father. He that honoureth not the Son honoureth not the Father which hath sent him.*

The Son Himself said that all men should honor the Son, even as they honor the Father. If Jesus were to be less than God, this would be a blasphemous statement. No ordinary man or prophet deserves to be honored as an equal to God Himself. God will not share His glory with a mere mortal man (not Moses, not Elijah, not Abraham, Isaac, or Jacob, not Peter, Paul, or John, not John Baptist, not Mary, not...). We could easily add Muhammad, Buddha, Joseph Smith, Mary Eddy

Baker, a Baptist preacher, pompous pope, Ellen White, and many others.

> **Isaiah 48:11:** *"For mine own sake, even for mine own sake, will I do it: for how should my name be polluted? and **I will not give my glory unto another**."*

There are liberal ministers (who love to call themselves "moderates") today that deny the Deity of Jesus. These religious hypocrites[3] do not even believe as much as the unsaved hypocritical Pharisees and the high priest who acknowledged Jesus' claim of being the **Son of God - (Mark 61-64; Luke 22:70-71; John 19:7)**.

Phony ministers refuse to honor Jesus Christ as The Son of God. They will readily admit that Jesus was a great teacher and prophet but deny His Deity. These pretending ministers of righteousness are deceitful workers and false apostles - (**2 Corinthians** 11:13-15; **I John** 4:13; **2 John** 7, 9-11). However, the day is coming when they will compelled to honor Jesus - (**Philippians** 2:10-11).

These false apostles may *appear* to be of us and be found even as we (2 Corinthians 11:12).

> **2 Corinthians 11:13-15:** *"For such are false apostles, deceitful workers, transforming themselves into the apostles of Christ. And no marvel; for Satan himself is transformed into an angel of light. Therefore it is no great thing if his ministers also be transformed as the ministers of righteousness; whose end shall be according to their works."*

The Workings of Satan and His Henchman

---

[3] **hypocrite**, Gk. hupokrite = stage actor; pretender of true religion

Christ and Antichrist Contrasted	
(by David W. Cloud)	

Christ	Antichrist
Humbled Himself ((Phil. 2:8)	Exalts himself (II Thes. 2:4)
The Good Shepherd (John 10)	The foolish shepherd (Zech. 11:16,17)
Exalted by the Father (Phil. 2:9)	Cast down to hell (Rev. 19:20)
Came to save (Luke 19:12)	Comes to destroy (Dan. 8:34)
Is the obedient one (Mk. 1:24; Phil. 2:7)	Is the lawless one (II Thes. 2:8)
Is the Truth (John 14:6)	Is a liar (II Thes. 2:10)
Came from above (Jn. 6:38)	Ascends from the pit (Rev. 11:7)
Did His Father's will (Jn. 6:38)	Does his own will (Dan. 11:36)
Came in His Father's name (Jn. 5:43)	Comes in his own name (Jn. 5:43) II Tim. 1:10; II Thes. 2:8; I Tim. 6:14; II Tim. 4:1,8;
The man of sorrows (Isa. 53:3)	The man of sin (II Thes. 2:3)
Despised by men (Isa. 53:3; Lk. 23:1)	Admired by men (Rev. 13:3,4)

Jesus is Greatly Honored in Heaven:

Revelation Chapter 5:

> *5:* "And one of the elders saith unto me, Weep not: behold, the Lion of the tribe of Juda, the Root of David, hath prevailed to open the book, and to loose the seven seals thereof.
> *6:* And I beheld, and, lo, in the midst of the throne and of the four beasts, and in the midst of the elders, stood

a Lamb as it had been slain, having seven horns and seven eyes, which are the seven Spirits of God sent forth into all the earth.
7: And he came and took the book out of the right hand of him that sat upon the throne.
8: And when he had taken the book, the four beasts and four and twenty elders fell down before the Lamb, having every one of them harps, and golden vials full of odours, which are the prayers of saints.
9: And they sung a new song, saying, Thou art worthy to take the book, and to open the seals thereof: for thou wast slain and hast redeemed us to God by thy blood out of every kindred, and tongue, and people, and nation."

Considering the following Scripture verse in John's Gospel, a beginner Bible student can easily identify **The Lamb in Heaven**:

John 1:29: "The next day John seeth Jesus coming unto him, and saith, Behold the Lamb of God, which taketh away the sin of the world."

The highest angel in Heaven cannot forgive sin! Neither can any man, whether he be a flaming Baptist preacher, devout Jewish rabbi, religious Catholic priest, pompous pope, strutting cleric, or any other titled person. Neither can any "so called" church authority save a man! Jesus alone saves. Jesus came to seek and save the lost (Matthew 18:11; Luke 9:56; 19:10). No one less than God can forgive sin.

The salvation of sinful humanity is referred to as "soteriology." Soteriology is the study of the divine accomplishment of the salvation of humanity as effected through Jesus Christ – (*Webster's New World College Dictionary*, Fourth Edition).

Jesus Was Slain That All May be Saved

> **Hebrews 2:9:** *"But we see Jesus, who was made a little lower than the angels for the suffering of death, crowned with glory and honour; that he by the grace of God should taste death **for every man**."*

There is no limited atonement here! Provision has been made that all might be saved, but all will not be saved (ye will not).

> **Revelation 5:6:** *"And I beheld, and, lo, in the midst of the throne, and of the four beasts, and in the midst of the elders, stood a Lamb as it had been **slain**, having seven horns and seven eyes, which are the seven Spirits of God sent forth into all the earth."*

(**Slain** is a sacrificial word. Jesus was God's Great Sacrificial Lamb! We see the precious **Lamb** numerous times in the book of Revelation - (**Revelation** 5:6, 8, 12- 13; 6:1, 16; 7:9-10, 14, 17; 12:1; 13:9; 14:1, 4, 10; 15:3; 17:14; 19:7, 9; 21:9, 14, 22-23, 27; 22:1, 3. The false prophet, the "Great Pretender" lamb, is seen in **Revelation** 13:11; 20:10.)

The born-again are redeemed by the shed blood of Jesus Christ, **The Lamb of God - Revelation 5:9** and **I Peter 1:18-19:**

> **I Peter 1:18-19:** *"Forasmuch as ye know that ye were not redeemed with corruptible things, as silver and gold, from your vain conversation received by tradition from your fathers; but **with the precious blood of Christ**, as of a Lamb without blemish and without spot."*

Any Person Who Is Unwilling
To Confess That Jesus Is God
Is Willingly Ignorant of the Scriptures:

> **I John 2:22-23:** *"Who is **a** liar but he that denieth that Jesus is the Christ? He is antichrist, that denieth the Father and the Son. **Whosoever denieth the Son the***

same hath not the Father: [but] he that acknowledgeth the Son hath the Father also."

The Anointed Messiah was Deity in flesh. Anyone relegating Jesus Christ to mere man or prophet and nothing more is denying the Father as well as the Son; he is of *the spirit of antichrist.*

Again and Again, Jesus is Confessed to be the Son of God in Scriptures:

Matthew 8:29	The **devils** confess
Matthew 16:16	**Peter** confessed it
Matthew 26:63	**Jesus** confesses it
Matthew 27:54	The **Roman centurion** is convinced...
Mark 1:1	**Mark** says so...
Luke 1:31, 32	The angel, **Gabriel,** says so...
John 1:34	**John Baptist** acknowledges...
John 1:49	**Nathanael** perceives...
John 6:69	**Peter** and the **apostles** believe...
John 11:4	**Jesus** plainly acknowledges...
John 20:31	**John** says so...
Acts 8:37	The **Ethiopian eunuch** believed...
Hebrews 4:14	The **writer of Hebrews** says so...
I John 4:14; 5:5, 20; 2 John 3	**John** repeatedly says so...

*Colossians 2:8-10: "Beware lest any man spoil you through philosophy and vain deceit after the **tradition** of men, after the rudiments (basic teachings) of the world, and not after Christ. For in him dwelleth all the fulness of the Godhead bodily. And ye are complete in him, which is the head of all principality and power."*

One major religion (Roman Catholicism) teaches that the Bible is not the sole authority but that their church **tradition** has equal validity along with other man-made dogmas and rituals:

- -sacerdotal mass - instituted by Cyprian – (3rd century)
- -prayers for the dead - (A.D. 300)

- -veneration of angels and dead saints and use of images - (A.D. 375)
- -mass - began A.D. 394 as a ritual (made obligatory 11th century)
- -extreme unction – (A.D. 526)
- -purgatory – proclaimed a dogma by the Council of Florence – (A.D. 1439)
- -prayers offered to Mary, dead saints and angels – (A.D. 600)
- -kissing the popes feet – (A.D. 709)
- -holy water, mixed with a pinch of salt and blessed by a priest – (A.D. 850)
- -canonization of dead saints, first by Pope John XV – (A.D. 995)
- -celibacy of priests declared – (A.D. 1079)
- -the rosary adopted from pagans by Peter the Hermit – (A.D. 1090)
- -the inquisition instituted by Council of Verona – (A.D 1184)
- -sale of indulgences – (A.D. 1190)
- -seven sacraments, defined by Peter Lombard – (12th century)
  - ➤ -auricular confession of sins to a priest instead of God – (Pope Innocent III, A.D. 1215)
  - ➤ -adoration of the wafer host – (Pope Honorius III, A.D. 1220)
  - ➤ -immaculate conception of Mary – (Pope Pius IX, A.D. 1864)
  - ➤ -tradition declared of equal authority with the Bible by the Council of Trent – (A.D. 1545)
  - ➤ -infallibility of the pope in matters of faith and morals proclaimed by the Vatican Council – (A.D. 1870)[4]

Note: Mary worship was established by Cardinal Benedetto Odescalchi, the first pope with the name of Innocent XI, when he initiated THE WORSHIP OF THE IMAGE, placed on the altar in 1677, and wanted his heart to be buried here, not in the main chapel. This is placed on a plaque in the Chapel of the Virgin of the Grace at Saints Vincent and Anastasius.

The Blood of Christ, Ordained of God...

[4] The above list of Roman Catholic inventions is taken from *Scriptural Truths for Roman Catholics* by Bartholomew F. Brewer, former Roman Catholic priest. Source *Way of Life Encyclopedia of the Bible & Christianity* by David W. Cloud.

- o -Justifies - **Romans 5:9**
- o -Unifies - **I Corinthians 10:16**
- o -Brings near to God - **Ephesians 2:13**
- o -Grants peace - **Colossians 1:20**
- o -Purges conscience - **Hebrews 9:14**
- o -Grants access to God's presence - **Hebrews 10:19**
- o -Sanctifies - **Hebrews 13:12**
- o -Cleanses from all sin - **I John 1:7**
- o -Frees from sins - **Revelation 1:5**
- o -Gives victory over Satan - **Revelation 12:11**

The Blood of God:

*Acts 20:28: "Take heed therefore unto yourselves, and to all the flock over the which the Holy Ghost hath made you overseers, to feed **the church of God**, which he hath **purchased with his own blood**."*

Speaking to the elders of the church, Paul names**...**

- o -the "Lord" once
- o -the "Lord Jesus" once
- o -our "Lord Jesus Christ" once
- o -the "Holy Ghost" twice
- o -"God" five times

"God is a Spirit" (John 4:24) and has no earthly body containing blood. Of course, it is **Jesus' blood** that was shed for sinners and with which God purchased the church of God. The Lord Jesus is named in verse 24; however, **God** is named in verses 24, 25, 27, and 28. Of course, we do not have to wrangle over this because the **Holy Ghost** and **Jesus** are **one in God - (I John 5:7)**. Since **Jesus is very God**, the church of God is purchased with **God's blood**.

The **trinity** of God is also beautifully shown here. The triune Godhead is found many times in Scriptures. As already stated, anyone denying the tri-unity of the Godhead would have to deny the trilogy of man's nature also.

> *Hebrews 4:12: "For the word of God is quick, and powerful, and sharper than any twoedged sword, piercing even to the dividing asunder of soul and spirit, and of the joints and marrow (body), and is a discerner of the thoughts and intents of the heart."*

The **body** (Greek "soma"), **soul** (Greek "psuche"), and **spirit** (Greek "pneuma") of man are frequently mentioned in Scriptures.

Actually, any religionist denying man's trinity could not believe in "life after death" because a part of that man, his body, remains on earth (without the soul and spirit). Again, man himself is a tripartite being made so by his Creator God.

> *I Thessalonians 5:23: "And the very God of peace sanctify you wholly; and I pray God your whole **spirit** and **soul** and **body** be preserved blameless unto the coming of our Lord Jesus Christ."*
> *Psalm 110:1: "**The LORD said unto my Lord**, Sit thou at my right hand, until I make thine enemies thy footstool."*
> *Matthew 28:19: "Go ye therefore, and teach all nations, baptizing them in the name of **the Father**, and of **the Son**, and of the **Holy Ghost**."*

Even "The Law of Probabilities" Proves That Jesus Christ is the Promised Messiah:

Mathematically, it can be proven to a reasonable person that Christ is the promised Messiah of OT prophecy. Of course, the probabilities of mathematics do not compare with the authority of **The**

Word of God. William W. Orr said in his booklet, **Can we Be Sure Jesus Christ Is God**:

> "If you were to measure the chance that over 300 differing prophecies would happen to converge on one man, the law of probability would demand a sum calling for more zeros that there are letters in all the words of an unabridged dictionary!"

Many Bible scholars and students say that there are 333 Old Testament Prophecies related to Christ's "First Coming."

Dave Hunt says:

> "The Old Testament contains more than 300 prophetic references to the coming Messiah that were fulfilled in the life, death, and the resurrection of Jesus. Sixty of these are considered to be major prophecies. If we eliminate 12 of these as within the power of Jesus and for His disciples to deliberately fulfill, that leaves 48. Professor Peter Stoner calculated the odds to be 10 to the 157th power that 48 such prophecies could be fulfilled by chance in Jesus Christ. In probability theory, it is generally agreed that any odds smaller than 10 to the fiftieth power are the same as zero. Since 10 to the 157th power is 10 to the 107th power (that's a 1 with 107 zeros after it) smaller than 10 to the 50th power, we can safely say that the fulfillment by Jesus of these 48 specific prophecies proved conclusively that He is the Messiah" --(Peace, Prosperity, & The Coming Holocaust, p. 100).

As one writer stated:

> "an incomprehensible mathematical monstrosity."

Only the God-man, the Lord Jesus Christ, could accomplish this.

Consider the Probabilities of these Astronomical Numbers:

❖ -The probability that one man could fulfill **one** prophecy in 300 is *"One in 300."*

❖ -The probability that one man could fulfill **two** prophecies in 300 is *"One in 90,000."*

❖ -The probability that one man could fulfill **three** prophecies in 300 is *"One in 27 million* ("One in 27,000,000").

❖ -The probability that one man could fulfill **four** prophecies in 300 is *"One in 8 billion/100 million"* ("One in 8,100,000,000").

❖ -The probability that one man could fulfill **five** prophecies in 300 is *"One in 2 trillion/430 billion"* ("One in 2,430,000,000,000").

❖ -The probability that one man could fulfill **six** prophecies in 300 is *"One in 729 trillion"* ("One in 729,000,000,000,000").

❖ -The probability that one man could fulfill **seven** prophecies in 300 is *"One in 218 quadrillion/700 trillion"* ("One in 218,700,000,000,000,000").

❖ -The probability that one man could fulfill **eight** prophecies in 300 is *"One in 65 quintillion/610 quadrillion"* ("One in 65,610,000,000,000,000,000").

❖ -The probability that one man could fulfill **nine** prophecies in 300 is *"One in 19 sextillion/683 quintillion"* ("One in 19,683,000,000,000,000,000,000").

❖ -The probability that one man could fulfill **ten** prophecies in 300 is *"One in 5 septillion/904 sextillion/900 quintillion"* ("One in 5,904,900,000,000,000,000,000,000").

The writer does not guarantee the accuracy of the above probabilities (not being a mathematician and unable to locate one with logistic skills) but the figures are certainly within the ballpark; neither has the writer attempted to locate all the 333 prophecies (he doesn't need to) relating to the Advent of Christ but is aware of about 100 of them.

Even if there were only 100 improbable prophecies fulfilled, the chances that only **ten out of the 100** being fulfilled would be, *"One in one-hundred quintillion"*

("One in 100,000,000,000,000,000,000").

"Who are kept by the power of God through faith unto salvation ready to be revealed in the last time."

1 Peter 1:5

CHAPTER 5

FULFILLED PROPHECIES

BY JESUS

Jesus Fulfilled the Prophecies of the Promised Messiah:

OT Prophecy	Reference	NT Fulfillment
Seed of a woman	Gen. 3:15	Gal. 4:4
Seed of Abraham	Gen. 22:18	Gal. 3:16
Born of a virgin	Isa. 7:14	Matt. 1:18
Lineage of Judah's tribe	Gen. 49:8-10	Mt. 1:3, 16
Born at a set time	Gen. 49:10	Luke 2:1
Born in Bethlehem	Mic. 5:2	Matt. 2:1
Heir to throne of David	Isa. 9:6, 7	Matt. 1:1
Time of His first coming	Dan. 9:25	Gal. 4:4
Innocent children slaughtered	Jer. 31:15	Matt. 2:17
Praised by little children	Psa. 8:2	Matt. 21:4, 5
Adored by great men	Psa. 72:10	Matt. 2:11
Proclaim a jubilee to the world	Isa. 58:6; 61:1	Luke 4:18, 19
Anointed with the Spirit	Isa. 61:1	Matt. 3:16
Heralded by John Baptist	Isa. 40:3	Matt. 3:1-3
Ministry began in Galilee	Isa. 9:2	Matt. 4:23
Dwell in Nazareth	Isa. 9:2	Matt. 2:23
A prophet like Moses	Deut. 18:15	Matt. 17:3; Jn. 1:17;

		3:14
Be a priest after Melchizedek	Psa. 110:4	Heb. 5:6; 6:20; 7:21
His ministry one of healing	Isa. 9:2	Matt. 4:15
Ministry of miracles	Isa. 61:1	Luke 4:18-19
Miracles not believed	Isa. 53:1	John 12:37, 38
Declared to be the Son of God	Psa. 2:7	Matt. 16:16; 27:43, 54
Preached in parables	Psa. 78:2	Matt. 13:34
Rejected by His brethren	Psa. 69:8	John 7:5
Betrayed by a friend	Psa. 41:9	John 13:18
Forsaken by His disciples	Zech. 13:7	Matt. 26:56
Sold for 30 pieces of silver	Zech. 11:12	Matt. 26:15
Disposal of His price	Zech. 11:13	Matt 27:7
Hand and feet pierced	Psa. 22:16	John 20:25
Garments parted and lots cast	Psa. 22:18	Matt. 27:35
Numbered with transgressors	Isa. 53:12	Luke 23:33
Made intercession for murderers	Isa. 53:12	Luke 23:34
Forsaken by God	Psa. 22:1	Matt. 27:46
Be the rejected Cornerstone	Isa. 53:1	John 12:37, 38
Rejected by the rulers	Isa. 6:10; Psa. 69:4	Matt. 15:8-9; Luke 20:17
Hated without a cause	Psa. 35:19	John 15:25
Be a man of sorrows	Isa. 53:3	Matt. 26:37, 38
Be dumb before his accusers	Isa. 53:7	Mt. 26:62; Mk. 15:3-5; John 19:9
Surrounded and mocked	Psa. 22:7-8	Matt. 27:39-44; Mk. 15:29-32
People sit and stare	Psa. 22:17	Matt. 27:36
Not a bone broken	Psa. 34:20	John 19:36
Buried with the rich	Isa. 53:9	Matt. 27:57-60
His resurrection foretold	Isa. 26:19	Luke 24:34
His ascension foretold	Psa. 68:18	Luke 24:51
Conversion of	Isa. 11:10	Acts 10:45

Gentiles unto Him		

More Prophecies:

OT Prophecy	Reference	NT Fulfillment
Out of Egypt have I called my Son	Hos.11:1	Mt. 2:15
Rachel weeping for her children	Jer. 31:15; 2 Kin 17:2	Mt. 2:18
He shall be called a Nazarene	Isa. 11:1	Mt. 2:23
He shall be called a Nazarene (a netzer or rod out the stem of Jesse)	Isa. 11:1	Mt. 2:23
The land of Zabulon & Nephthalim saw great light	Isa.9:1-2	Mt. 4:12-16
Bruised reed and smoking flax	Isa. 36:6; 42:1-4	Mt. 12:20
The King cometh upon an ass and a colt	Zech. 9:9	Mt. 21:4, 5
Healed all the sick	Isa. 53:4, 5	Mt. 8:16; 9:35; 12:15; 15:30
My house shall be called the house of prayer	Isa. 56:7	Mt. 21:13
Out of the mouth of babes and sucklings thou has perfected praise	Psa. 8:2	Mt. 21:16
They parted my garments...cast lots	Psa. 22:18	Mt 27:35
Be scourged, spit on, hair plucked, cheeks smitten	Isa. 50:5	Matt. 26:67; 27:30; Mk. 14:65
They shoot out the lip, they shake the head	Psa. 22:7; 109:25	Matt. 27:39
Friends would stand afar off	Psa. 38:11; 88:8; Isa. 63:3	Luke 23:49
He would agonize with thirst	Psa. 22:15; 69:3, 21	Luke 23:49; John 19:28
Willingly gave up His	Isa. 50:6; 53:12; Dan.	Matt. 20:28; John

life	9:26	10:11, 18
His heel bruised	Gen. 3:15	Matt. 27:34-35; Luke 23:33, 39
Die with malefactors	Isa. 53:12	Matt. 27:44; Luke 23:33, 39
His body would not disintegrate	Psa. 16:10	Acts 2:27
Dying words foretold	Psa. 22:1; 31:5	Matt. 27:46; Mark 15:34
Cut off	Dan. 9:26	John 3:16; I Cor. 15:3, 4
Crucified Christ hidden by darkness	Amos 8:9; Psa. 22:2	Matt. 27:45
Become a greater high priest than Aaron	Psa. 110:4	Heb. 5:4-6, 10; 7:11-28
He would be seated at God's right hand	Psa. 110:1	Matt. 22:44; Heb. 10:12, 13
His rejection followed by destruction of Jerusalem and great tribulation	Dan. 9:27; 11:31; 12:1	Matt. 24:15; Mark 13:14
The Spirit of the Lord... upon me	Isa. 61:1, 2	Luke 4:18-21
Jesus read this Scripture in the synagogue and applied it to Himself. Word of God forever	Isa.40:8; Psa 12:6, 7	Mt. 24:35; Luke 21:33

QUESTION:

Is there any human being of Jewish ancestry (**Genesis 12:1-3; 28:10-15**) of the tribe of Judah (**Genesis 49:10**) and of the family of David (**2 Samuel 7:16; Jeremiah 23:56**), born in Bethlehem (**Micah 5:2; Matthew Matt. 2:16**) to a Jewish virgin (**Isaiah 7:14; Matthew 1:23**) and who was despised and rejected by his own brethren (**Isaiah 52:13, 14; 53:1-9**) and died being innocent (**Luke**

23:41; 2 Corinthians 5:21) and all of this <u>before the destruction of the Second Jewish Temple</u> (**John 2:19, 20**)?

The Luminaries Preach Christ and Redemption:

The book of Job, which is probably the oldest book in the world, refers to the constellations of the solar zodiac:

> ***Job 9:9:*** *"Which maketh Arcturus, Orion, and Pleiades, and their chambers of the south."*

Even before the Holy Scripture was given to man on earth, the heavens declared the glory of God (**Psalms 19:1**) in "star-pictures." Before Abraham's time, Job referred to the Mazzaroth, or Constellations of the Zodiac (**Job 38:32**).

The Book of Job is not only the oldest Book in the world, it is also considered the most scientific book of the Bible.

The star-pictures of the Zodiac (in the beginning of creation) were prophecies in the heavens concerning Christ, His wounded heel (Christ's sufferings for our sin), conquest of Satan (Christ wounding Satan's head), redemption for man (Calvary), and Christ's eternal Kingdom. Of course, the Constellations have been grossly **mis**-interpreted and counterfeited by astrologers, corrupt religion, humanism, and classic mythology. It is **not** hard to figure out the symbolism of "Leo the Lion," "Virgo the Virgin," nor "Hydra the Serpent."

Even **a star of wonder** heralded the birth of Jesus, the King of the Jews, to the Magi in the East **(Matthew 2:1, 2).** God garnished the heavens with groups of stars that send the greatest message of all time (The Gospel of God's grace in the person of His Son, Jesus Christ) to all men everywhere. Even a fool should be able to reason that the star-designs of heaven loudly and majestically declare the greatness and glory of God. Remember too, a fool in Scriptures is not someone who is mentally deficient. The Bible fool is an unbeliever who is proud, spiritually blind, stubborn, and independent of God (sound like anyone you have heard of or seen).

Could Christ Have Sinned?

This subject is usually referred to as "The Impeccability of Christ." (**Impeccable** = not capable of sinning or liable to sin; free from fault or blame; flawless – *Webster's Ninth New Collegiate Dictionary*.)

Jesus was indeed a man, but unlike other men He had **no sin in Him**. The writer of **Hebrews 4:15** says that our High Priest (**Jesus--Hebrews** 4:14-15), as a man (**...**made like unto his brethren - **Hebrews 2:17**), could be touched with the feelings of our infirmities "yet without sin" or "apart from sin."

> ***Philippians*** *2:6-8: "Who, being in the form of God, thought it not robbery to be equal with God: But made himself of no reputation, and took upon him the form of a servant, and was made in the likeness of men: And being found in fashion as a man, he humbled himself, and became obedient unto death, even the death of the cross. Having been made in the form of a man, He suffers with us when we suffer. In our temptations, there is enticement or temptation from indwelling sin; but Jesus was never enticed that way for there was no indwelling sin in Him. Jesus was tested outwardly."*

Some object by saying that one who is unable to sin cannot really be tempted...

➢ You can test *pure gold* all you want to, but it still remains pure gold (without any slag, dross, or impurities).

➢ You can assault an *impregnable* barrier with a mighty force but it will remain unscathed.

> ➢ You may attempt to break an *unbreakable chain* with great tensile strength but it will remain unbroken.

<u>Jesus, our High Priest, could be tested but without sin:</u>

> ***Hebrews 4:14-15****: "Seeing then that we have a great high priest, that is passed into the heavens, **Jesus the Son of God**, let us hold fast our profession. For we have not an high priest which cannot be touched with the feeling of our infirmities, but was in all points tempted like as we are, yet **without sin**. When Jesus had fasted forty days and forty nights in the wilderness and was afterward an hungred, the devil tempted Him three times - (Matthew 4:1-11). Jesus, in a weakened body of earthly flesh, overcame the devil's testing."*

William L. Pettingill said:

> "If Jesus had failed under the test and yielded to the temptation of Satan, that would have proven, not that God in the flesh could sin, but rather that Jesus of Nazareth was not God in the flesh."

Pettingill adds:

> *"If we say that the Lord Jesus could have sinned while upon earth, how can we deny that He might sin even now up in Heaven?"*

> ***James 1:17****: "Every good gift and every perfect gift is from above, and cometh down from the Father of lights, with whom is no variableness, neither shadow of turning."*

<u>Does James 1:13 say that God cannot be *tempted*?</u>

<u>Answer:</u> Yes. However, the plain statement has to be considered within its context (some were claiming that God had *tempted* them).

(**NOTE:** The meaning of *temptation* closely resembles *testing* though there is a difference.)

> **James 1:13:** *"Let no man say when he is tempted, I am tempted of God: for God cannot be tempted with evil, neither tempted he any man:"*

Again, neither God nor His Son Jesus has any indwelling sin with which to be tempted. The context of the verse in James 1:13 relates to transferring the cause (not the guilt) of the sin to another (just like Adam blamed Eve and Eve blamed the serpent). It appears that some had excused their sin by claiming that God had tempted them beyond their capacity to resist - (**James** 1:13, 14). **Tempting to sin does not come from God**. To tempt to sin is contrary to the holiness of God. No one can charge sin to God; God does nothing to tempt man to sin. Man is tempted when he is drawn away of his own lust, and enticed. God allows or sends trials (not sin temptations) to make a believer better in his graces, not to corrupt him with sin temptation. God is not the author of any man's sin.

Jesus, being God in the flesh, could not be tempted within: He was tested without.

Jesus never ceased being God in His body of flesh, but He did set aside His heavenly glory and subject Himself to humanity, *"... was in all points tempted like as we are, **yet without sin**."* - (**Hebrews** 4:15). It cannot be over stated, Jesus could not sin because He never ceased to be God...even in His body of flesh!

CHAPTER 6

CONCLUSION

Jesus said, _"I am Alpha and Omega, the first and the last..."_ (Revelation 1:11). Jesus is the central theme of the Bible. Jesus said in John 5:39, _"Search the Scriptures...and they are they which testify of me."_

The prophecy of **Psalms 22:16** (written about 1,000 years before Christ) says _"...they pierced my hands and my feet."_ This is a prophecy of Christ's crucifixion. The suffering Savior is also prophesied in **Isaiah 53:7 and Daniel 9**. Crucifixion was unknown then and was not invented until hundreds of years later. Crucifixion came into its earliest use with the Phoenicians, Greeks, Carthaginians, and Romans. Emperor Constantine, the first official pope (pontifex maximus), did away with it in about 325 A.D. (No, Peter was not the first pope!)

Jews and Evidently Some Samaritans Knew of the OT Prophecy of the Coming of Messias

> **John 4:25-26:** _"The woman saith unto him, I know that Messias cometh, which is called Christ: when he is come, he will tell us all things. Jesus saith unto her, **I that speak unto thee am he.**"_

Jesus affirms that He is the promised Messiah. The adulterous Samaritan woman met the Water of Life at Jacobs well (John 4:14).

Even the Tree of Christ's Crucifixion is Referred to in Typology of the OT:

> *Exodus 15:25:* *"And he (Moses) cried unto the LORD; and the LORD shewed him a tree, which when he had cast into the waters, the waters were made sweet: there he made for them a statue and ordinance, and there he proved them."*

The fulfillment ("antitype") of the OT **tree** (type) is referred to several times in the New Testament. Of course, the literal fulfillment is recorded in the four Gospels.

> *Acts 5:30-31:* *"The God of our fathers raised up Jesus, whom ye slew and hanged on a tree. Him hath God exalted with his right hand to be a Prince and a Saviour, for to give repentance to Israel, and forgiveness of sins."*
> *I Peter 2:24:* *"Who his own self bare our sins in his own body on the tree, that we, being dead to sins, should live unto righteousness by whose stripes ye were healed."*
> *Acts 13:29-30:* *"And when they had fulfilled all that was written of him, they took him down from the tree, and laid him in a sepulcher. But God raised him from the dead."*
> *Galatians 3:13:* *"Christ hath redeemed us from the curse of the law, being made a curse for us: for it is written, Cursed is every one that hangeth on a tree."*

The bitter sufferings of Christ upon the **tree** (the wooden cross) is God's offering for our sins (**John** 3:16; **2 Peter** 3:9) and sweetens the sorrows of our lives.

All Scriptures Testify of Jesus:

> *"Search the Scriptures...they testify of me (Jesus)"* - ***John 5:39***
> *"He (Moses) wrote of me (Jesus)"* - ***John 5:46***
> *"Abraham rejoiced to see my (Jesus') day; and he saw it, and was glad"* - ***John 8:56***
> *"Before Abraham was, I AM (Jesus)"* - ***John 8:58***

John 1:1-2, 14: "*In the beginning was the Word, and the Word was with God, and the Word was God. The same was in the beginning with God. And the Word was made flesh, and dwelt among us, (and we beheld his glory, the glory as of the only begotten of the Father), full of grace and truth.*"

Psalms 110:1: "*The LORD (God the Father) said unto my Lord (God the Son), Sit thou at my right hand, until I make thine enemies thy footstool.*"

John 8:24: "*I said therefore unto you, that ye shall die in your sins: for if ye believe not that I am he, ye shall die in your sins.*"

Romans 10:13: "*For whosoever shall call upon the name of the Lord shall be saved.*"

God Laid Down His life For Us

The love of God is expressed in that He died for us, in the person of His Son, the Lord Jesus Christ. And we ought to lay down our lives for the brethren.

I John 3:16: "*Hereby perceive we the love of God, because he laid down his life for us: and we ought to lay down our lives for the brethren.*"

Again, God laid down His life for us. All genuine Christians believe in the Divinity of Christ. Even many unsaved people believe that Jesus is God in the flesh (however, a sinner must repent of his sin and plead the mercy of God for salvation). The general agreement of the cults is in the denial of the absolute Deity of Christ Jesus and it is not accidental.

No person that ever lived in the entire world, but Jesus Christ, could answer to the 53rd chapter of Isaiah:

Isaiah 53:3-6: "*He is despised and rejected of men; a man of sorrows, and acquainted with grief: and we hid as it were our faces from him; he was despised, and we esteemed him not. Surely he hath borne our griefs, and carried our sorrows: yet we did esteem him stricken, smitten of God, and afflicted. But he was wounded for our transgressions, he was bruised for our iniquities: the chastisement of our peace was upon him; and with his stripes we are healed. All we like sheep have gone astray; we have turned every one to his own way; and the LORD hath laid on him the iniquity of us all."*

Isaiah 44:6: *"Thus saith the LORD the King of Israel, and his redeemer the Lord of hosts; I am the first, and I am the last; and beside me there is no God."*

These two persons of the Trinity are saying in unison, *"...beside me there is no God."* Both the Father, as King of Israel, and the Son, as the Redeemer of men, speak here as one and declare their unity and Deity.

Revelation 22:13: *"I am Alpha and Omega, the beginning and the end, the first and the last."*
This is the glorified Christ speaking.

Luke 13:3: *"I tell you, Nay: but, except ye repent, ye shall all likewise perish."*
Ephesians 2:8-9: *"For by grace are ye saved through faith; and that not of yourselves: it is the gift of God: Not of works, lest any man should boast."*
Romans 10:9-10, 13: *"That if thou shalt confess with thy mouth the Lord Jesus, and shalt believe in thine heart that God hath raised him from the dead, thou shalt be saved. For with the heart man believeth unto righteousness; and with the mouth confession is made unto salvation. For whosoever shall call upon the name of the Lord shall be saved."*
Matthew 11:28-30: *"Come unto me, all ye that labour and are heavy laden, and I will give you rest. Take my yoke upon you, and learn of me; for I am meek and lowly in heart: and ye shall find rest unto your souls. For my yoke is easy, and my burden is light."*
John 3:36: *"He that believeth on the Son hath everlasting life: and he that believeth not the Son shall not see life; but the wrath of God abideth on him."*

John 8:24: "I said therefore unto you, that ye shall die in your sins: for if ye believe not that I am he, ye shall die in your sins."

The Two Comings of Christ

In theological circles, the two comings of Christ to earth are usually referred to as "The First and Second Advents of Christ."

In the First Advent: Jesus came the first time to seek and save the lost (Luke 19:10). This was possible because Jesus died as a sacrifice for sinful man. God's holiness demanded a perfect sacrifice and Jesus was the only one that could pay the supreme price for sin. Jesus made the way of salvation possible between a Holy God and sinful man and man only has to repent and plead the mercy of God through God's provision for his sin (Luke 13:3; John 3:16; Ephesians 2:8, 9; Romans 10:9-10, 13; Matthew 11:28).

Philippians 2:6-8: "Who, being in the form of God, thought it not robbery to be equal with God: But made himself of no reputation, and took upon him the form of a servant, and was made in the likeness of men: And being found in fashion as a man, he humbled himself, and became obedient unto death, even the death of the cross."

In the Second Advent: As certain as Jesus' First Advent is His future Second Advent. However, at His Second Advent, he does not come as a lamb to the slaughter, but He comes as King of Kings and Lord of Lords in great and terrible judgment of the world and sinners. The cup of iniquity of the Gentile nations is full and running over. The Gentile nations will be judged at this time and Israel will be purged.

Revelation 19:15-16: "And out of his mouth goeth a sharp sword, that with it he should smite the nations: and he shall rule them with a rod of iron: and he treadeth the winepress of the fierceness and wrath of Almighty God. And he hath on his vesture and on his *thigh a name written, **KING OF KINGS, AND LORD OF LORDS**."*

Repentance and Salvation for the Sinner is Only Promised for Today, and No More.

2 Corinthians 6:2: "(For he saith, I have heard thee in a time accepted, and in the day of salvation have I succoured thee: behold, now is the accepted time; behold, now is the day of salvation.)"
John 8:24: "I said therefore unto you, that ye shall die in your sins: for if ye believe not that I am he, ye shall die in your sins."

These words of Jesus were spoken to the religious and unbelieving Pharisees of Judaism but the same message is applied to all who reject His Deity. The reader can plead the mercy of God today but is not promised tomorrow.

Sleep well tonight because it could be your last night upon earth! Remember, there is no Second Chance, middle ground, limbo state, or purgatory.

*Luke 12:16-21: "And he (Jesus) spake a parable unto them, saying, The ground of a certain rich man brought forth plentifully: And he thought within himself, saying, What shall I do, because I have no room where to bestow my fruits? And he said, This will I do: I will pull down my barns, and build greater; and there will I bestow all my fruits and my goods. And I will say to my soul, Soul, thou hast much goods laid up for many years; take thine ease, eat, drink and be merry; But God said unto him, Thou fool, **this night thy soul shall be required of thee**: then whose shall those things be, which thou hast provided?"*

Will a Man "Exchange" His Soul for Worldly Gain That He Cannot Keep (Most Will)?

Matthew 16:26: *For what is a man profited, if he shall gain the whole world, and lose his own soul? Or what shall a man give in* **exchange** *for his soul?*

John 4:48: *Then said Jesus unto him,* ***Except ye see signs and wonders, ye will not believe.***

Dennis Helton
200 Home Place Drive
Easley, SC 29640

"...not with enticing words of man's wisdom"

I Corinthians 2:4 -(KJB)

"All that the Father giveth me shall come to me; and him that cometh to me I will in no wise cast out. For I came down from heaven, not to do mine own will, but the will of him that sent me. And this is the Father's will which hath sent me, that of all which he hath given me I should lose nothing, but should raise it up again at the last day. And this is the will of him that sent me, that every one which seeth the Son, and believeth on him, may have everlasting life: and I will raise him up at the last day."

John 6:37-40

INDEX

About the Author

The writer was born in Greenville, SC in 1934 and was a lifetime resident with the exception of two years in the US Army (Fort Jackson, S.C. and Fort Carson, Colorado) and two years residence in Florida.

After separation (honorably) from the US Army, the writer returned to Greenville, SC and married at age 27 to Christine Moore, an old acquaintance from an adjacent neighborhood. The Lord blessed us with six daughters, Debbie, Donna, Dale, Denise, Deree, and Dena.

A short time after marriage, the writer was convicted of his lost condition as a sinner and after a miserable time under conviction the writer confessed his sin and lost condition to God and was saved.

The writer was 40 years of age when he began attending college (3 years, no diploma).

The writer retired as a chemical technologist from Morton International Chemical Company in 1996. Before retirement, the writer had the urge to write on Bible subjects and wished that he had more time to study. Upon retirement, the writer bought a computer and became a novice writer.

The writer now resides in Easley, S.C.

"Beloved, now are we the sons of God, and it doth not yet appear what we shall be: but we know that, when he shall appear, we shall be like him; for we shall see him as he is."

1 John 3:2

www.ingramcontent.com/pod-product-compliance
Lightning Source LLC
Chambersburg PA
CBHW062005040426
42447CB00010B/1928